Forward

I met Mark while windsurfing in the beautiful waters of the Peel estuary. Externally Mark presented as the consummate elite athlete, he's big and strong and consistently performs at the elite level. Mark was always generous with his time and was prepared to share whatever resources he had. Fortunately for me, after some of our exhilarating windsurfing sessions, I got to have some deep and meaningful conversations with Mark which revealed that underneath the powerful athletic exterior was a sensitive and thoughtful man who had endured significant emotional trauma throughout his life.

This book describes Mark's journey of resiliency through loss and grief. It is an account of that journey. It's raw and its unsanitized, and you get the messiness of it all. Basically, what you hear in a counselling session when someone is truly spilling the beans. I think it's one of the things you have to do to fully heal. While I was reading the book I began to recognize that his story was almost a textbook clinical account of psychological resiliency, which mirrored the work I do that encourages people to undertake in trauma recovery work. In Mark's book you get it raw and real, with insights on what an authentic journey of healing looks like in reality. It's not a step-by-step instruction manual of a self-help book.

If I was to undertake a thematic analysis of Marks book about resilience in the face of grief and loss; I would find what the research on resiliency has found. Psychological research will tell you that resiliency comes from a deep sense of meaning, from changing the internal narrative about yourself and your life, from undertaking physical activities/practices which re-regulate the autonomic nervous system, from having achievable goals and realistic time frames, from making deep human connections with trustworthy people and from being unafraid to ask for help when you need it. Mark's raw account of his journey of healing is what this book is about. In a way the book is about what recovery from a life of emotional trauma actually looks like in real life.

Paul Alexander - Senior Mental Health Consultant

Separated Fathers Recovery

www.separatedfathersrecovery.com

First published by Separated Fathers Recovery 2025

This edition published 2025 1

Copyright © 2025 by Mark Woodley

Mark Woodley asserts the moral right to be identified as the author of this work

A catalogue record of this book is available from the National Library of Australia

ISBN: 978-1-7641645-0-4

DON'T DIE DAD

A Separated Father's Journey from
Devastation to Peace and Acceptance

Dedicated to the well-being of
separated fathers and their kids

Mark Woodley

AUTHOR'S NOTE

This memoir is built upon a meticulously-kept record of events spanning more than a decade. Throughout my separation and the years that followed, I maintained a detailed archive of every text message, email, and letter exchanged. These records formed the factual foundation of this narrative, allowing for a clear and accurate chronology of events. More importantly, they gave me the space to explore the emotional truth behind those moments—reflected upon with the perspective and insight that only time and healing can offer.

To protect the privacy of those involved, the names of individuals have been changed.

I want to make it clear: I love my children no more and no less than their mother does. My ex-wife is a devoted and capable parent who has also endured the immense pain that comes with separation and divorce. She and I consciously and subconsciously made decisions that hurt each other and our children immensely. Our children love their mother deeply and wholeheartedly, as they should—despite how circumstances unfolded, and it is my most heartfelt wish that this never changes. Just as I hope they always know my love for them remains unwavering and unconditional.

ACKNOWLEDGEMENTS

To my dear, loved children:
Who endured a fractured adolescence and carried the undeserved burden of parents unable to preserve the stability you once knew. I love you both unconditionally and beyond these words. I honour your strength.

To my valued and loved sister:
Thanks for your life-long acceptance, love and understanding me.

To Michaela:
Thank you for the love you gave so freely. You were always innocent, and I will always be grateful for what we shared.

To my windsurfing mates:
My tribe. Without your support, these words would never have found the page. Thank you for catching the wind with me when I had none in my sails.

To Andrea:
Thank you for your loyalty, friendship, and support.

To Lucas:
For listening and providing a framework for healing over these past few years.

To my ex-wife:
Thank you for the times of joy with our kids. I wish you absolute health and happiness.

TABLE OF CONTENTS

AT THE CROSSROADS

A decade ago, I stood on a busy Perth city street, gazing at a text message that would dramatically alter my life as I knew it. My ex-wife and I were not blameless in what ensued, but responsible for the trauma inflicted on our children and each other. We both made decisions—some for survival, some out of pain or fear, and a few in vengeance. As I look back now, I see two people who lost the vision of compromise in marriage, who went back to their own worlds rather than battling for middle ground for the benefit of family. The business I created was the lifeblood of our once financially rich world but provided an absent cohesive outlook for the family's legacy. It became a barrier between us in time, just as her desire for social escape drew her further away.

The ten years that followed transformed everything. My role as a husband disintegrated. My position as a father evolved into something I never predicted. The thriving business, our home and family, the future we'd once envisioned—all of it changed into something unfamiliar, and in many forms completely unrecognisable. I saw my son Luke look away, my daughter Olivia's universe shatter. My ex-wife's actions at various times after separation to control, influence and restrict my contact with our kids agonised me beyond comprehension at times, yet I had to discover that anger would not fix what was shattered.

I fought addiction—alcohol to numb the pain, gambling to chase lost security. Twice I've stood at life's edge, thinking an end would be easier than beginning again. But this is not a story of blame or victimisation. It's a story about how we need to persevere when the path we planned shatters and disappears. When we find strength not despite our failures, but because of what they teach us.

I am not drafting this book to instruct anyone on how to live his or her own separation and divorce—every shattered family does what it can with the wreckage. But if you are in the position I was in, perhaps my story can offer you what I most needed then and many times throughout the tortuous journey: evidence that you can survive and find a sense of peace and acceptance. That you can start over at the bottom. That being a different kind of father does not have to mean being a worse one but adapting into a new variant of what the new life circumstance allows.

The tale that follows unfolds over the span of three days in the New Zealand Southern Alps. Among the unforgiving rocky slopes, jagged cliffs, and the attempts on a rugged summit, it threads its way through a decade of learning the lessons of letting go, toughening up, and staying open-hearted after bruising and deciding to adapt to a new life. There are no neat answers here, no ten-step plan for ideal post-divorce parenting. An honest reflection on what it means to completely lose your way, to experience a loss so profound it's beyond comprehension, to fail and still find the strength to rise again, to love your children so deeply that you're willing to reinvent yourself and your life when circumstances demand it.

These pages contain my truth—not as a victim or hero but as an ordinary man and loving father who passed through the fire and emerged scarred, unrecognisable in parts, and transformed. If my experience will provide at least a faint light to guide at least one other separated father who has faced, or will face, the same darkness, then its telling will have been worth every painful word.

Keep climbing.

Mark Woodley

1

THE GREEN LIGHT

A return to my Nirvana and the text message that changed everything

All this time since the text message that destroyed my life, and I still couldn't delete it from my mind.

My thumb hovered over my phone as I sat on a granite boulder halfway up a New Zealand mountainside like it had ten years ago.

The words glowed accusingly: *I wish things were different, but I think you will be happier in time...*

My bitter laugh echoed off the slate-gray rocks.

Happier, without my kids and traditional father identity.

Right.

And so, I was here alone at fifty-two, muscles aching, sweat evaporating on my scalp despite the chill mountain air. The Southern Alps lay ahead of me like a barrier of bastions, their serrated peaks heaving upwards through veils of cloud.

Beyond the rolling mists, somewhere above were things I wasn't certain I wished to discover. But a force within had taken me there unwilling for debate.

My spiral notebook was open on my black daypack, its crisp white pages waiting to capture whatever insight the mountain was willing to impart.

The craggy face of the mountain mirrored the landscape I'd fallen in love with fifteen years before—jagged peaks tearing into clouds, valleys lush with stunning green pastures, lakes mirroring blue so bright it seemed artificial. This was the paradise I'd once hoped my children Luke and Olivia would call home, where they might have ridden their bikes along scenic mountainous trails instead of learning to navigate the broken landscape of split homes.

My trekking poles stood at attention, waiting patiently for the next push upward. Like the blank pages of the notebook, this mountain presented a clean slate, an opportunity to re-author my life, to find meaning in an existence I was unsure of its current purpose.

Then, I continued to hike up the gruelling, uneven terrain. Loose scree and fractured stone create an unforgiving path beneath my feet. I had to be careful— a wrong step would be deadly. Less painful to concentrate on where I put my feet than on how vacant my house was now, how Luke had found a lengthening distance from his once super dad, how I'd had to release custody of my dear Olivia that final time and how my fiancé had packed up and left.

"Need a break?"

I was startled by the voice. A few meters along the trail, a young man was looking at me with an inexplicably familiar expression. He had the sort of open face that stirred a distant memory—something from long ago that I couldn't quite place, the sort of face that still radiated positivity. The scuffed hiking boots and plain daypack indicated someone who knew these trails.

"Going to the summit?" he asked, eyes crinkling at the corners as he smiled. Something in that smile gave me pause, stirred a memory I couldn't quite reach.

I glanced up at the cloud-obscured peaks. "I'm not sure I'll make it that far. I'm just seeing where the trail goes."

"Mind if I join you for a while? I'm Jonas." He walked alongside me as we climbed on. "I'm not in a hurry to get to the top, and you look pretty steady. You don't seem to be in any rush. Besides, the views are too stimulating and meant to be savoured, not raced by."

My muscles groaned with each step. Six years of battling winter storms and summer afternoon squalls on my windsurfer, chasing the strongest winds nature provided, had started to restore my strength, but this was a completely different kind of terrain. The slopes of the colossal mountain in the Southern Alps shone randomly beneath the pewter sky below us. The same landscape that had stolen my heart fifteen years before, when we'd visited as a family of four—before I still dared to hope to give my children the life they deserved.

"Why are you in New Zealand?" Jonas inquired between careful breaths after hearing my Australian accent.

The question struck harder than the sharp edges of shattered scree pushing into the side of my hiking boot. My chest constricted as the memories came flooding back: standing on a busy Perth city street, looking at that never-ending text message that took continual scrolling to read until the end, my legs weakening even as some primal survival mechanism carried me along, hauled me on even as my world was collapsing around me.

"I always wished to live here," I said at last. "Had it all figured out—ten acres of land, wonderful schools and activities amongst nature. Leave the rat race behind forever. Now I've come back to find out if there's still room for me and to see if it still feels right, like it once did."

Four months earlier, I'd sent one final letter of goodwill to Wayne, the man who'd been raising my children with my ex-wife. I copied Luke, Olivia, and my ex-wife, making my intentions clear—I just wanted to meet him, to find some peace about the man who'd stepped into the role I once filled. When Olivia, unguided and influenced beyond my short phone conversation, innocently dismissed my efforts and Wayne rejected my goodwill a second time—four years after my first attempt—something inside me broke. The final nail in the coffin of my fatherhood. That rejection drove me back to these mountains, searching for direction other than my primal father role. My natural and chosen purpose in life.

"Family then?" Jonas's voice was soft, coaxing.

"Two children. Luke and Olivia." Their names stuck in my throat. I had not said them aloud in days, let alone in conversations with them. "We were going to make a life here. But their mother had other ideas…"

I drew back, my hand instinctively moving to reach for my phone concealed beneath my shirt pocket. Certain scars never completely heal—they simply become a part of you.

"I recall precisely where I was when I received the message," I said to Jonas, pausing my upward steps and running my fingers over the textured face of a large granite rock near us. "Center of Perth's business district. Friday afternoon. There was a Giants parade in town—streets filled with families, kids on shoulders, all faces turned upwards towards these enormous wooden puppets winding through the city."

The memory slammed into me with physical force.

On that day, I stood motionless in the middle of Perth's heaving business district, an island of paralysis in a sea of celebration. The Giants parade surged around me, a kaleidoscope of colour and noise that barely registered through the shock. Enormous puppet heads bobbed meters above the crowd, their manic grins mocking my private agony. Children shrieked with laughter, their small hands *clutching their parents and some waving both stretched arms up at the giants. Parents hoisted squirming toddlers onto shoulders, pointing eagerly at the spectacle as they paraded the city centre.*

And cutting through it all, searing and insistent, the vibration and buzz of my phone in my hand.

With sweating fingers, I pressed the message alert and saw a message titled "Dianne my wife." I opened Dianne's text, the words blurring before my eyes after reading the first sentence.

"Hi, I wish so many things were different, but I think you will be happier in time. Gabrielle Symonds agreed that a trial separation is the best way forward…"

Each phrase sliced into me, a multitude of bullets each piercing through my heart. My knees buckled, and for a moment, I thought I might collapse right there on the sidewalk, trampled beneath the oblivious horde. But some instinct kept me upright, locking my joints even as my mind reeled.

…she gave me some great advice to stay living together for at least 2 weeks, preferably four. not tell the kids until we are less upset and can tell them calmly together…

The kids. Oh god, Luke and Olivia. The thought of them twisted like a knife in my gut, doubling me over, instantly churning my gut into sickness. They were somewhere in this crowd, weren't they? I thought their schools would have had an excursion and I may see them in the horde somewhere where their innocent faces would be tipped up to the sky, drinking in the magic, unaware that their world was about to shatter. I didn't want them to see their father doubled over in the sea of celebration and slowly stood tall again feeling semi-conscious, trying to comprehend the space between reality and a wishful dreamscape.

Yet, I knew what was coming. Knew it in my blood and bones, with the certainty of a man who'd watched his own family splinter apart as a teenager. The bewilderment, the rage, the helpless thrashing against a pain too big to understand.

I instantly saw it all stretching ahead of them, an endless road of broken promises and fractured holidays, of shuttling between houses, divided loyalties and learning not to ask for what they needed.

And I'd thought I could save them from it. That's why I'd clung so fiercely to the dream of New Zealand—to the sun-drenched fields and mountain-shadowed schools, the promise of a better life uprooted and replanted. I'd encouraged Dianne through open homes and schools, painting pictures of the future we could grasp, if only she'd reach out alongside me.

As I stared at that tiny screen, the hopeful fantasy crumbled like sand through my fingers.

...do you think this will work for you? I love you so much it's just so sad that our compatibility doesn't work...

The words swam before me, blurred by the hot pressure building behind my eyes. Compatibility. As if a fifteen-year marriage, a shared home, two miracle children, could be reduced to a single metric. As if our life together was an equation that no longer computed, an outdated device to be traded in.

Around me, the parade raged on, a surreal backdrop to my personal apocalypse. Music pounded from huge speakers, base drums boomed, wooden arms swung marching parading with medieval red-costume clad assistants coordinating the giants' movements. The smell of a crowd's energy and hot asphalt mingled, filling my nostrils. I felt like I was choking on it, on the innocent cheer, the wilful blindness to the bomb that had just detonated in my chest.

I wanted to scream until my vocal cords frayed. I wanted to grab the strangers streaming past and shake them, make them look into my face and witness the wreckage. Couldn't they see that my world was ending? Couldn't they taste the ashes from the incineration of my family in the air, the bitterness flooding my mouth?

But of course, they couldn't. To them, this was just another hot sun-soaked afternoon, another cheerful parade in a city drunk on its own booming mining fortune. My personal hell was nothing more than a passing blip, a forgettable smudge on the margins of their carefree lives.

So, I swallowed the howl rising in my throat, the animal anguish threatening to claw its way out. Blinked back the tears that blurred the final, damning lines.

So hard to press send so sad

For a single, wild second, I almost laughed. Hard to send. Where was I supposed to dredge sympathy for Dianne's tender feelings? She'd just ripped the heart out of our family, shattered everything I'd spent a decade and a half building, and she wanted me to acknowledge how difficult it was for her?

The urge to put my fist through the nearest wall was sudden and overwhelming. To scream until the sky cracked open. To crumple to my knees and let the crowd swallow me whole, kicking and writhing as I disappeared beneath their feet.

But even as the impulses shredded through me, I felt my traitorous legs carrying me forward, my body a machine operating independently of its master. The crowd buffeted me, their laughter abrading my skin like sandpaper. Suddenly, I couldn't bear it—the relentless joy, the taunting normalcy of a world that no longer made sense.

So, I did the only thing I could. I turned to escape the physical intensity and mental torture. Not running in case of collapse should my heart stop in protest of what was already shutting it down.

Shouldering through the mass of revellers, the crush of bodies swallowed me, the noise and colour blurring into a smear. My feet pounded the pavement, carrying me away from the gigantic puppets, the cheers, the life I'd known.

Towards a future I could barely stand to contemplate. My pace increased to a run as the crowd was left behind, fighting my heart's caution until my lungs burned, my vision blurred, with the taste of salt sharp on my lips.

Perth fell away behind me, garish and oblivious. Ahead, the horizon stretched bleak and uncharted, a wasteland littered with the shards of everything I'd dreamed.

My children's faces flashed before me, distorted as if underwater. Olivia's giggle warped into a sob; Luke's grin crumpled like a used tissue. The last traces of their innocence, already slipping away.

There'd be no protecting them now, no shielding their tender hearts from the fallout. The text message had made sure of that.

The carnival music faded, drowned out by the rasp of my breath, the drumbeat of my pulse in my ears. But even as the parade receded, I couldn't outpace the knowledge of impending carnage searing through me.

My family was gone, incinerated by a single text. And rising from the ashes, unstoppable as the tide, the gates of hell gaped open, hungry, and waiting.

All I could do was try not to let them drag me under.

---------------•●•---------------

"The text ended with how hard it was to press send," I told Jonas as we walked. "How sad she was. But she'd already made up her mind. The trial separation was just theatre. I figured that out later. The evidence indicated that she had emotionally withdrawn. I just didn't know it yet."

Jonas studied my face. "How long before you stopped checking your phone for that message?"

When I met his eyes, I saw something there that made my chest tighten. "I deleted it from my phone that night after saving it for as one day it may serve as the beginning of truth for my kids. There's still an imprint of it on my heart, where two spots are for my kids."

He smiled gently, understanding. "And now here you are. Hiking to find answers in the mountains."

"Something like that." I squinted up at the jagged summit, still so distant, wreathed in mist. "When everything was falling apart, I kept coming back to New Zealand. Dreaming about what could have been. Wondering if I was wrong not to fight harder for it." I shook my head. "Pathetic, right?" I was struck by how easily I found comfort in speaking so honestly to this stranger walking beside me.

"Human," Jonas corrected. He tilted his head, considering me. "But you know what I think? I think you're looking in the wrong place for permission."

I frowned. "Permission?"

"To let go. To start over." He gestured at the sweeping vistas around us. "You think you'll find it out here, but the truth is, you already have it. Your ex-wife gave it to you the second she sent that text."

His words settled like sharp stones in my gut. I stared over the valley, watching clouds cast shadows on the distant peaks.

"She offered me a green light," I said slowly. "And I was too scared to take it. Not without my kids. The choice felt unbearable—between a new life in New Zealand without them or staying behind to fight through the complexities of shared custody and the emotional toll of watching them navigate life between two homes. It felt like a no-win situation. If I left, I feared I'd be abandoning them. If I stayed, I knew the emotional strain might unravel everything. I chose to stay. Of course I did. I could never leave them. But somehow, despite staying, I still lost them. Just more slowly, and more painfully."

"Is the light still green?"

The question hung in the thin air. My mind unable to articulate the thoughts of possibility or not.

———————·••·———————

A week after the separation, I found myself caught in a dizzying whirlpool of emotions, swaying from despair to cautious optimism and back again. It was as if my heart couldn't decide which reality to inhabit—the bleak certitude of divorce or the fragile possibility that this was all just a terrible misunderstanding.

I clung to that latter hope with a desperate intensity, replaying Dianne's message in my mind, parsing each word for hidden meaning. A trial separation, she'd called it. Didn't that imply an end point? A chance to repair what had broken?

I pictured us sitting down with the counsellor Dianne had mentioned, laying our cards on the table, working to untangle the knots we'd tied ourselves in over the years. In my mind's eye, I saw Dianne's face softening, her hand reaching for mine in front of the polished Mari timber expanse of the therapist's desk. A recognition dawning in her eyes—that what we'd built was worth fighting for, that our family, our kids, were more than the sum of our incompatibilities.

But even as the fantasy played out, I could feel the cold breath of reality on the back of my neck, the insistent tug of grief in my belly. Because deep down, in a place I could barely stand to acknowledge, I knew the truth.

The words "trial separation" echoed in my mind like a lifeline—but over time, I began to sense that it wasn't a pause, but an ending softened by careful language. Maybe it was meant to protect us both from the pain of the truth. Maybe it was just how people let go—slowly, kindly, and at a distance. Dianne had already made her choice—I'd heard it in the tone and finality of her words, felt it in the space between each careful line of text. Our marriage was over, had probably been over for longer than I cared to admit. And no amount of couples therapy or tearful reconciliations or heartfelt poetry could change that fundamental fact.

The realization would hit me at odd moments: driving to work or standing in line at the supermarket. A wave of nausea, a cold sweat prickling my hairline. The phantom buzz of my phone in my pocket, an eerie echo of that awful day at the Giants parade.

I'd think of Luke and Olivia, their sweet faces shadowed with confusion as Dianne, and I stumbled through the awkward dance of separation. The halting explanations, the forced cheerfulness as we promised them that nothing would change, that we'd still be a family even if we weren't living under the same roof.

But everything had already changed, and we all knew it. I saw it in the way Luke's eyes shuttered when I entered the room, his preteen moodiness calcifying into something harder, more impenetrable. I saw it in the lost look on Olivia's face as she watched Dianne pack an overnight bag, her stuffed pink teddy clutched to her chest like a life raft.

The guilt was a living thing, clawing at my insides. I knew I should be handling this better, providing a steady anchor for my kids to cling to in the churning seas of divorce. But half the time, I felt like the water was seconds away from suffocating me in a moment of weakness.

Some days, the anger was a welcome respite from the grief, a righteous flame burning away the cobwebs of despair. I'd channel it into work, throwing myself into projects with a manic intensity, as if I could somehow prove my worth through sheer productivity. Other times, I'd let it loose on the first convenient target—a barista who burned my coffee, a red light that caught me at the wrong moment, a telemarketer unlucky enough to dial my number.

But beneath the fury, always, the yawning chasm of loss. The knowledge that the life I'd designed and perhaps taken for granted had vanished overnight, replaced by a bleak and uncertain future.

And then, like a cresting wave, the hope would surge again, offering a sliver of light in the darkness. I'd replay the happier scenes in my head, grasping at each shred of joy like a drowning man clutching driftwood. The memory of Dianne's laugh, unguarded and effervescent, on that long-ago trip to New Zealand. The mornings I'd woken to the smell of pancakes wafting up the stairs, Olivia covered in flour and Luke sneaking chocolate chips from the bag. The pride in Dianne's eyes on the day we'd signed the purchase on our dream home, the one I'd thought would be ours forever.

Looking back now, I see those moments for what they were—flashes of light in a slow, inexorable dimming. But in the raw aftermath of Dianne's revelation, they felt like a lifeline, a flimsy thread tethering me to the world I'd known.

——————————•●•——————————

"Hey, you, okay?"

Jonas's prying voice yanked me back to reality.

"Yeah, what did you say?" I asked, my footsteps crunching against the rocky earth as I hiked up the path.

"Are you still afraid to take the green light?" Jonas asked again.

Forcing the thought of which was all a blurry haze, I thought of the last decade— the acrimony, the custody issues, the weathering of relationships, the slow erosion of everything I'd built. The way Luke's eyes once could only endure my presence and Olivia retreated into silence. The hollow ache in my bones as I rattled around my new house that felt so empty with just me rattling around in it.

And beneath all of it, buried deep: a kernel of something bright. The vision I'd nurtured 15 years ago, travelling through these same mountains, gazing up at their sharp peaks in wonder, dreaming of the day I'd finally climb and hopefully live amongst them. A different life. One of space, light, and laughter.

A life that could still be mine. If only I was brave enough to claim it.

I met Jonas's eyes. Felt something shift inside me, a tectonic plate locking into place.

"I don't know," I said. "I just don't know," I repeated, wishing I could say "yes," with a sense of conviction.

He raised an eyebrow, sensing the tension in my voice. "What's going on?"

I sighed, my shoulders slumping. "When my last attempt to make things work with Wayne failed, I had to face the truth. I've been replaced. The man my kids are growing up has substituted me; my kids don't need me anymore. My dear daughter doesn't get why I need this closure as she's influenced by forces that have shut me out."

There was a long pause before he spoke again, his tone light but understanding. "So, what now?"

"I need to figure out if I can build a life here alone," I confessed. "Now that I know I'm no longer needed there, I need to know if there's a future for me somewhere else. Somewhere where I feel a connection and energy to finally rebuild into a new person detached with amnesia from the past."

He grinned, giving me a friendly clap on the shoulder. "Well then, let's keep climbing. We'll see where these slopes take us."

We shouldered our packs and stepped forward on the loose scree, the distant summit glimmering above us like a promise. As we climbed, I tasted the possibility of renewal in the wind, sharp and clean as snow.

The sun caught the brim of my hat as I paused to catch my breath, the alpine lake a brilliant turquoise jewel far below. From this vantage point, the world looked different. Problems that had seemed insurmountable at the valley floor now appeared as small as the scattered stones beneath my boots. The thin air at this altitude stripped away pretense, leaving only what was essential. Like the clouds drifting across the jagged peaks behind me, I too was in a state of constant motion, searching for solid ground and somewhere to call home.

Maybe the time was finally right. Maybe I could still find my way to the life I'd glimpsed all those years ago.

The life I was always meant to live.

Standing on that rocky outcrop, I felt the first stirrings of something I hadn't experienced in years: possibility. The white cotton of my shirt caught the mountain breeze, and for a moment I was reminded of my windsurfing sail ready to catch the wind which would propel me to a feeling of freedom. The heavy clouds above mirrored my own turbulent thoughts, but through them, shafts of sunlight broke through—nature's reminder that even the darkest skies eventually clear. I wasn't at the top of the mountain yet, but I had come this far.

2

THE SPEECH

Telling the children their family was breaking up

The granite face rose before us, a profile of weathered stone edged in gold by the afternoon sun. My boots scraped against the loose scree as we rounded another switchback, making a purposeful crunching sound mirroring my determination to keep grinding on. That's when I saw it: an incredible rock formation that seemed to be a perfect heart, balancing precariously on the mountain's edge.

Jonas stopped too, hitching his worn canvas pack higher up his shoulders. Sweat darkened the collar of his worn hiking jacket as he stared at the impossibly stubborn stone heart. It was resisting gravity, perched easily in the middle of clear mountain air, having survived countless seasons of wind, rain, ice, and snow that had stripped these mountains bare over millennia.

"Stubborn little thing," Jonas reflected, wiping his forehead with a faded red bandana. "Sitting up where it shouldn't." He ran a finger along one of the more substantial veins in the rock, following the path where minerals had crystallized ages ago. The healing was irregular, the stone knitted in a way that told of surviving at any price."

"Nature finds a way to adapt," I rasped, my throat gravelly from both the altitude and the memories weighing on my chest. Long shadows crept across the granite as scattered clouds drifted overhead. "Even when everything is against it."

"Not always gracefully, though." Jonas's hand fell from the weathered stone. A chill breeze swept around us as the crunching sound of gravel radiated under our hiking boots. "Sometimes surviving means being shaped by pressure, transformed by heat and time."

My throat tightened as the past roared forward, ferocious as an avalanche: our sun-filled kitchen with granite countertops, stainless steel appliances, and glass dining table, Luke's and Olivia's faces aglow in the warm light of pendant lamps and late afternoon sun, pizza boxes piled between us like a fragile tower against what was to come. The words I had practiced a hundred times faded on my tongue.

"Sometimes survival is lying to yourself," I told Jonas, the confession grating raw awakening from their wanting retreat. "Pretending everything will be okay, even when you know better. Tell yourself there's hope in your heart." I shook my head, not able to continue.

He tilted his head to one side, waiting with that unsettling patience I was growing to know. The wind paused as a car-sized granite boulder briefly sheltered us, and we were enveloped in mountain silence.

"I had to tell my children their family was breaking up." The words fell like stones in that quiet. "I tried to smile as I told them to conceal the tragedy I was unfolding. I told them it would be better this way. That we'd all be happier." I let out a sarcastic laugh. "What sort of father tells lies to his children like that?"

The mountain air thinned around me as I dove into that night, the weight of the memory bearing down upon my lungs.

---•●•---

The pizza was Olivia's selection—supreme with double olives. She picked them off one by one and placed them in a line at the border of her plate as Luke inhaled his second slice. The ordinariness of the scene cut deep: Friday evening dinner in our sunny dining area, fading light casting through the white-painted timber bifold doors we'd recently installed. A photo from the life I was going to ruin.

My hands trembled as I gripped the paper, meticulously selected words blurring before my eyes. Beside me, Dianne was wearing her favourite blue sweater, impeccably dressed except for her white-knuckled grip on her knife and fork. We had spent hours crafting this speech, arguing over every word until each sentence gleamed with unnatural perfection.

"Hello, guys." My voice was stronger than I had hoped, letting out an artificial optimism. "Mum and Dad have discovered how to be even better parents to you and even better friends to one another."

Luke's slice hovered halfway to his mouth. Olivia just kept segregating her olives into tidy piles, and her head tilted in gentle interest.

"You know how Mum and I have been away for a week and then back to you guys for the last few months?" The words I had practiced were razors in my mouth, cutting with every lie I spoke. "And we've still been doing things with you and sometimes all together—like rides, dinner out, shopping?"

Two little nods. My chest tightened.

"We believe we can be better parents if we do it that way, so we will continue living separately." The rehearsed words tumbled from my mouth, each one of them a further betrayal. "Everything will be just the same as it has been for these past few months. You guys remain here, and Mum and I will have the same amount of time with both of you, one week at a time."

I made myself glance into their eyes, hunting for traces of the destruction I knew was imminent. But Luke just looked at his pizza briefly before putting it down. Olivia took a sip of her drink, completely unfazed.

"When we were together all the time, we fought too much, and it kept us from being happy and from being the best parents to you guys." The lies tasted metallic on my tongue with the only truth being told, "It's not your fault at all that we fight too much, so you are not at all to blame."

At the time, I genuinely believed we were working toward something—that this so-called "trial separation" might be the beginning of our reconciliation. I didn't yet understand that things had already shifted.

It was only much later, while reviewing the call records from my company phone, that I noticed something that stayed with me: a late-night conversation the same evening my grandfather passed away. That night, I'd driven Dianne to a family friend's house with Luke and Olivia still in their pyjamas. She was heading out to a comedy festival for a birthday celebration with her mothers' group. I had no reason to doubt anything then—it all seemed normal. But looking back, with the clarity only time and distance can bring, I began to see that a new connection— emotional or otherwise—may already have been forming. And I was no longer part of that unfolding story.

"We both love you so much equally and think your awesome kids. Mum and I have had lots of long grown-up talks about this, and we have received some fantastic assistance from counsellors, individuals that we trust." More make-believe, cleverly written to ease the pain. "We have had mixed emotions about carrying on living apart and you might feel the same."

Luke scooted his chair back, pizza forgotten. Olivia's olive soldiers remained at attention, awaiting commands that would never be given.

"We are here for you one hundred percent, twenty-four hours a day, and whatever you're feeling is normal, okay, and we'll comfort you." My voice shook slightly.

"Whatever questions you need to ask are important to us and we'll answer it honestly."

The irony of promising honesty while burying them in lies wasn't lost on me.

"We also have many friends who have supported all of us, so we are not alone." I pressed on, desperate to reach the end. "Mum and I actually think we can be better to each other this way which will make our relationship even better and, therefore, be better to you guys."

Luke stood up, stretching casually still chewing. Olivia's eyes followed him, her attention already receding from this world-changing moment.

"So, Mum and I love each other deeply and will make it as simple and normal as it has been." The final lies, the heaviest ones. "So, from your point of view, no real change from the last two months but just happier, fun times with both of us. We'll still be doing our things together as a family like our riding, school functions, movies, dinners, shopping, footy, and soccer games."

They were already heading towards the door to the manicured yard, Arnie's tail wagging as he trailed along behind them. The dog's enthusiasm for playtime effectively eclipsed the seriousness of what had happened.

"Go on," I struggled, seeing them disappear outside into the waning light. Their laughter drifted back through the windows as they wrestled with Arnie the Shiatzu Poodle on the lush freshly cut lawn, the world already coming back together around them in a way it never would for me.

I sat at the vacant table, gazing at half-consumed pizza and discarded olives, while the precarious facade dissolved.

I'd escaped upstairs afterward, my legs just managing to get me to the ensuite before I'd fallen. The tiles were cold against my face as I'd struggled to hold in the sobs leaking from what had just shattered me. All the terror I'd felt since my own parents split had washed over me:

It was after dinner that I went to the garage to clean my bike. A second-hand racing bike I had bought with my casual job earnings cleaning at a local factory. Mum and Dad had a turbulent relationship that saw Mum with bipolar disorder until she was then diagnosed with Motor Neurone Disease in her late fifties. My father had a second stroke unbeknownst to me a few months before the evening he confronted me about my mum. The result was him walking up to me in the garage that evening with a sombre face. One that I rarely saw but knew would deliver serious news. As I continued to clean the wheel spokes, he stood over me and said, 'Mark, a man will be coming from the court next Tuesday at 5pm. He will hand your mother a form which will indicate she must leave the house permanently. She will have one week to move out. You can either go with her or stay here.' I kept cleaning the spokes I had sprayed degreaser on in shock, unable to look up at my dad. My arm and hand continued independently of my mind which catapulted into a daze of confusion, despair, anger, and grief all within a second of hearing Dad's words. My next thought was that I would stay. This was my home. Where I had my dog, rode to school and the beach to windsurf. My mates were close and the unknown with Mum didn't get a thought of acceptance.

The feelings lying on the tiles, the anger, the confusion, the slow poison of split holidays and divided loyalties. The way childhood fractures into "before" and "after," never again whole.

I knew this world intimately and I'd vowed I'd never put my kids through what I'd gone through. And there I was, just moments from reading the same damned play my father had read from, reciting the same ending of a family message but using different words. The freshly painted white timber bifold doors opened to a stunningly landscaped garden with pool of which the kids immersed themselves in daily, the photos on the walls, the whole life we'd constructed; everything collapsed as our kids ate pizza and played with the dog, unaware they sat in the rubble.

Sunlight poured in through the window visible from the ensuite floor, casting a glow over the wedding photo on the bedroom wall—a younger me beaming for the camera, praying I'd never do to my own kids what had been done to me. At least my father had been honest, not spoken from a meticulously crafted message of false hope. I had been watching my family disintegrate while our children played outside, oblivious to the fact that they were playing in the discards of their parents' relationship.

———————·•·———————

"I didn't know at the time," I told Jonas, my hand resting on the cool rock, "that her growing preference for time with friends—even on nights that used to be sacred for us as a family—signalled a deeper shift I couldn't yet see. I honestly believed this 'trial separation' was just that—a pause, a chance to reset. It felt official, wrapped in the language of a professional, and that gave me hope we were working toward something. Rebuilding."

"God, what an idiot," I added, the words catching in my throat. "I remember writing poetry back then—lines that pleaded with her to reconsider, to soften. I was desperate to evolve, to keep us together, to fight for the glimpses of harmony we once shared parenting Luke and Olivia. There were moments of real joy. But by then, the tide had already turned. I just didn't know it yet."

"You protected the kids the only way you could," Jonas whispered as if to console me but loud enough to hear. A cloud shadow crossed us, momentarily diffusing the harsh mountain sunlight.

"Did I?" I sniggered bitterly. "Or did I make it worse by pretending? By letting them think there was hope when I should have been bracing them for the truth?" I smiled wryly. "Or perhaps I compounded it by playing along? By allowing them to believe there was hope when I ought to have been preparing them for the truth before the speech of lies. They were not fools—they saw through it eventually. Made it worse when the truth finally struck." I thought of my father's separation message thirty-six years ago as being one of simplicity and honesty. I felt an admiration for this approach whilst apparently sick and despite the fact he removed my mother from the constancy of my adolescent life.

"They were too young to handle the whole truth," Jonas contended. "Sometimes protection means covering up the light, allowing it in little by little instead of all at once."

"Perhaps." I moved away from the rock, boots grinding on the loose rocky trail. Some spilled over the edge and fell away into nothing slipping from under my boot. "But I was too afraid to deal with it myself. Too afraid to deal with what was going on. If only we'd have gone to New Zealand when I'd wanted." I let my voice fade, the old regret as bitter as trail dust in my mouth.

Jonas regarded me with those disquietingly knowing eyes—eyes that appeared to bore straight through my defended walls to the scared father within. "Is that why you've come back here? Searching for courage?"

"Possibly." The word got caught in my throat. Clouds flowed over the peak above, revealing and hiding the peak in a play of shadow and light. "I'm not sure I know what I'm searching for anymore. I was a hands-on passionate father and a successful businessman. And now I just windsurf to feel alive. I feel incomplete and lost at 52."

"Let's just keep climbing, then," Jonas said matter-of-factly. He shifted his pack straps with a comfortable familiarity. "The mountain has a way of revealing what you need to see, even if it's not what you're seeking."

We buckled on our packs and ascended higher, leaving the balanced heart shaped rock to its solitary vigil allowing the wind to touch us again as we hiked on. But its image stayed with me—weathered but steadfast, defying gravity in perfect balance, finding stability on the unforgiving mountainside. Its mass had settled perfectly enough to secure it against storms that would have toppled less balanced rocks.

Maybe that's all any of us can do when the ground shifts beneath us: anchor ourselves, withstand the pressure, and reshape to endure. Even if it means cracking along the way. Even if it means letting go of the form, we once believed was unbreakable.

The faded trail steepened ahead of us, demanding attention with shifting rocks ready to slide down the near vertical mountain side with the slightest step too forceful. But my mind lingered with that rock, with its stubborn defiance of gravity and its beauty. Standing guard over the distant valley like a sentinel, bearing witness to all the ways we break, transform, and endure.

Not always gracefully. But somehow, still standing.

3

THE SHATTERED PATH

Navigating the early aftermath of separation

A rockslide had blocked our path at one point, sending sharp wreckage across the steep faintly marked trail.

Recent, from the new scars ripped into the mountainside above. The granite slivers sparkled in the afternoon sun—some fist-sized, others car-sized, all wrenched from their ancient anchors by forces beyond their control precariously sitting ready to shift again without warning.

Jonas kneeled beside a fractured boulder, tracing the crystalline veins revealed by its forceful breaking away from the cliff face. The rough edges glittered in the light, transforming ordinary rock into something nearly lovely in its fractured state.

"Nature has its own timetable for falling apart," he stated, straightening up with a grunt. His boots ground smaller fragments beneath his feet as he walked nearer to the cliff. "Sometimes even granite boulders they'll hold together for millions of years, then crack apart in a second."

The air was crisp and pure, fitting for such a stunning environment. Below us, a lake was like burnished obsidian under sparse white clouds. The destruction had provided a new panorama of the valley—unplanned but dramatic.

"We'll have to find another way up," I said, looking for alternative routes up the rocky cliff face. The main route was now buried beneath tons of debris that had fallen some fifty meters above.

"Or admit that this is where we end today." Jonas plopped down on a reasonably substantial granite rock just large enough for a single seat, removing his pack. Sweat marked the back of his old green jacket despite the mountain chill. "Sometimes the path you planned isn't the path you take."

My jaw clenched at his words. I could barely see through breaks in the wreckage field where the trail picked up again on its twisting ascent. So near, and yet now completely inaccessible. The mountain had rearranged our plans without our prior consent.

"Odd how that works," I said, the bitterness spilling out despite myself. "You spend years mapping the perfect route, so confident you know exactly where you're headed. And then one day..."

"Everything comes crashing down?" Jonas completed softly.

I looked out at the devastation before us—the broken stone, the impassable trail, the altered landscape. The metaphor was not lost on me.

"The initial Sunday custody trade was like this," I found myself saying. "Standing in my own driveway, watching my children jam their backpacks into their mother's car. Everything I thought I knew about my life, being a father—just gone. Lost beneath the weight of this new reality I never wanted nor felt deserved.

A desired house in an affluent neighbourhood, a present father, holidays around the world, love and affection, fiercely dedicated and loyal to my kids and wife."

The recollection struck with physical force, keen as the mountain air searing my lungs.

————————————•●•————————————

That first Sunday. Four in the afternoon.

I was standing in the driveway of what had been our family home, the sun beating down on immaculate pavement and a manicured lawn where Luke and Olivia had once rolled Olivia's pushcart and Luke's skateboard together. Sometimes they would both scrunch up together and ride the red pushcart laughing in delight. Dianne and I had once been great parents—before my business stress, unresolved traumas and growing distance took their toll; before Dianne's nights out with her friends and my ignored inputs to our future plans became more common than family movie nights and her listening to me; before we retreated into our own worlds instead of fighting for middle ground.

These days, the children crept from house to house with bulging backpacks, their childhood glee traded for guarded quiet. We'd instructed them in that, Dianne and me—how to navigate around grown-up conflicts, how to get by in the no-man's land between two damaged individuals who'd forgotten how to meet halfway.

"We need to talk about money," Dianne said, her voice tight with a tension we both had long grown accustomed to. She leaned against the kitchen bar, already dressed to head out, just as I had once buried myself in work as a way to cope. In truth, my business had become a refuge—a place where I felt autonomous, away from the emotional undertow we couldn't name or fix.

As things deteriorated, our separation seemed to take on a life of its own, driven by legal frameworks that felt less like protection and more like strategy. With ample resources between us, we had once lived comfortably— Dianne had embraced the role of full-time mother, a choice I'd supported and enabled. I encouraged her trips to Melbourne with the kids, believing that maintaining connections with her family and lifelong friends would enrich Luke and Olivia's world.

That night, the kids sat quietly on the couch, watching something far beyond their understanding unfold. None of us had imagined this future for them. And yet, here it was. I moved toward them, hoping to salvage something gentle from the storm.

They ran to me—Luke hesitant, Olivia holding my hand tightly, her little fingers shaking. It was a kind of heartbreak I would relive weekly, etched in hugs and Sunday goodbyes. The air between Dianne and me was thick with things unsaid, but our children felt every word we didn't speak.

I whispered, "Not now," trying to suspend the inevitable for just a moment longer— for their sake.

But the pattern had already taken hold. The same tense handovers, the same quiet withdrawals, the same way our children were learning that love can unravel even in the nicest of homes. The haven we built had become a place for two lives lived in parallel—never quite intersecting, never quite healed.

We'd promised ourselves we would be different than our own parents. But here we were, unintentionally showing Luke and Olivia how a family could come apart. We split their lives down the middle, convinced we were giving them equal love in equal time, not realizing that our best intentions still left them with a fractured whole.

I'd built my business around being a hands-on father—school drop-offs, pickups, soccer practice, dance classes, bikes in the cul-de-sac, dinners on the patio. The garden bloomed around them, the red fountain spilling into a pool framed by Frangipanis. It was the life I believed in. The life I thought we'd all chosen.

Jonas brushed granite dust from his weathered hiking pants.

"There's usually another way up," he said, squinting at the cliff face and ready to climb once more. "If you're willing to look for it."

The broken trail disappeared under the rockslide, but a faint track curved away to our left—treacherous, rougher, barely more than a goat path sketched into the mountainside. Dark clouds gathered above the peak, promising afternoon rain.

"Might be smarter to turn back," I said, but my dusty hiking boots were already moving toward the new path. The first few steps sent loose rocks skittering into space.

Jonas followed, his boots finding purchase where mine slipped. "Sometimes the harder path is the only one left."

We picked our way up the treacherous incline, using handholds where the track narrowed to inches. Every step required absolute focus. One wrong move meant a long fall into the valley below. My immediate thought was of my passport, zipped securely in the top section of my pack, in case identification was required because of one accidental slip.

"Like learning to be a different kind of father," I said, testing a rock before trusting it with my weight. "When you can't be the one you thought you'd be."

A bitter gust whipped around us, carrying the first cold drops of rain. The crude path grew steeper, demanding more from muscles already burning with fatigue. Each step felt like a fight against gravity itself.

"Had to let go of being Super Dad," I continued, the strained words coming harder than the climbing. "The one who was always there. Who could fix anything. Who never let them down."

The route curved sharply right, bringing us to a narrow ledge. Below, the valley floor seemed impossibly distant, and above, the peak vanished into darkening clouds.

"Luke saw it first," I said. "The moment the cape came off..." Circumstance removed it from me, leaving only a wounded and broken father inept of any admiration. My thoughts directed to Luke proudly giving me a Father's Day card.

Luke's handmade card captured the truth of how he once saw me, a superhero in his eyes. The blue cartoon figure with a red cape, standing tall, was me to him then: invincible, dependable, his guardian. The childlike scribble of "Daddy my Hero!" with stars sprinkling the background was both a cherished memory and a painful reminder of the character I was no longer grasping. That card, so full of real respect from an era prior to our world's splitting asunder, was wealth and torment— memory of what was lost when the cape dropped off.

———————————•●•———————————

The ping pong table—that had been our thing. Luke would race home from school for years, already calling out a challenge before his backpack hit the floor. We'd play for hours, and our matches got more competitive as he grew. I'd taught him how to put spin on the ball, and how to read his opponent's shots, and shared all the tricks I'd learned in my youth with my dad. The steady rhythm of the ball bouncing between us, his face lit with fierce concentration, our scorekeeping getting more vocal as his skills and winning became regular.

Then one day, he stood in the doorway of my rental house, that familiar challenge absent from his voice. The table waited in its usual spot; paddles were laid out with the care of ritual.

"Want to play?" I asked, already knowing the answer from his closed expression.

"No." Flat, final. He didn't even look at the table, this centrepiece of so many afternoons together. Just walked past it to sprawl on the couch, phone already in hand.

The next morning, I stood staring at that green surface, seeing not the present but all those disappeared moments—Luke's victory dances, his running commentary, the way he used to lean in to the spin of each serve, and his bursts of laughter that would leave us in disbelief of some of our amazing shots. Luke told me he was playing with Wayne at his mother's house, creating new memories I wouldn't be part of.

Without fully forming the thought one morning after returning from the school drop off, I gripped the edge of the table. In one fluid motion, I tilted it on its side. The legs folded with a snap that echoed through the empty house. I carried it out in one piece, impatient to remove it from future possibility of torment. It felt like removing a shrine to something already long gone.

The table hit the curb with a dull finality. No ceremony, no rage—just the deeply saddened acknowledgment that some chapters end whether we're ready or not.

Luke's final departure came a few years later without ceremony.

I stood at the kitchen sink, washing dishes from a dinner I'd carefully prepared, hoping home cooked wagyu burgers might bridge the growing silence between us. The sound of the front door slamming shot through the house. No words, no warning—just the hollow bang of finality.

I dried my hands and walked to the front door past the kitchen bench, where I picked up my phone to see a message. "Come get me." It must have been sent to his Mum and me.

After all the careful custody arrangements, legal battles, and negotiations, my son's exit came down to this: a slammed door and a plain text. From one hundred percent custody to zero in the space of a heartbeat.

The dishes stayed half-washed in the sink, steam slowly rising from water starting to cool. I could feel his suffering and frustration but was unable to hug and console him as Super Dad, once could.

———————— •●• ————————

"Luke," I gripped the rock face harder, the memory catching in my throat. "We used to do everything together—mountain biking out in the hills, repairing remote control cars in the garage, footy on the street, movie nights with Olivia and Arnie sprawled across the carpet."

A crack of thunder rolled across the peaks. Jonas waited, letting the silence stretch between my words.

Random drops of rain then broke out of the thick clouds as we hugged against the cliff face. The narrow route was becoming slick and treacherous, each step a negotiation with gravity. Jonas pressed his shoulder into the rock wall, creating an anchor point against the wind.

"Up there," he shouted over the gusty wind, pointing to where the crude route rejoined the main path about thirty meters above. "We can still make it."

I squinted through the drops hitting my eyes. The route looked impossible—worse than what we'd already climbed. But going back meant navigating this knife-edge in reverse.

"Sometimes the only way is forward," Jonas said, as if reading my thoughts.

It was challenging to find my balance as we continued. The rock was wet and rough under my feet, but solid. Like the day I'd finally accepted that my relationship with Luke had to change before it could heal—if it ever would.

"You know what I learned?" I called out, my voice nearly lost in the wind. "You can't force someone to walk beside you, not even your own child. Sometimes, loving them means letting them find their own path, even under the influence of others, like the man they live with."

I thought of how Olivia used to brush against me while walking. She wasn't trying to push me, but feel my constant support and guidance. Now, she walked at a distance—if at all—choosing instead to remain at home with Arnie the dog during our last times living together. It felt like she didn't need me anymore.

Has Wayne taken my role, I wondered?

Jonas nodded, thick drops hitting his face. "Even if that path leads away from you?"

"Especially then." I pulled myself up another few feet, muscles burning. "But you keep climbing anyway. Keep your own footing solid. So, if they ever look back..."

"They'll know where to find you," Jonas finished.

Strong wind gusts buffered us as we pressed against the cliff face.

The narrow ledge offered scant protection from the wind now working to a fury.

Each strengthening wind gust threatened to tear us from our precarious perch.

"The worst part wasn't losing the everyday moments," I said, voice barely carrying over the wind. "It was knowing someone else got to have them instead."

Jonas braced himself against a jutting rock, eyes squinting as the wind blasted a few raindrops into his exposed face. "Wayne?"

The name hit like a physical blow. "Dianne's new partner. The man who sleeps under the same roof as my children—who gets to see them every morning, hear about their days, watch them grow." My fingers dug into the stone hand holds until they ached. "Who, at the time, took my spot playing table tennis with my son."

A savage gust whipped between us. Jonas steadied himself before speaking. "That must burn deep."

"You have no idea," I said, the words catching in my throat. "Watching your own children—their DNA, your legacy—be raised in a life you're no longer central to. An unknown man to me sharing the everyday moments I once lived for. Breakfasts, bedtime routines, family holidays, restaurant dinners… being present in all the small ways that used to be mine. All while I remained a visitor in their lives, confined by custody orders and awkward transitions."

My voice cracked. "For Olivia especially, it was harder. She was so young, so impressionable. I worried how she might make sense of the shifting roles and loyalties around her. At that age, children look for safety, affection, approval. I could only hope that in the complexity, she still knew who I was—Her real dad. That my love didn't vanish just because I was no longer with her."

Shards of light split the sky, illuminating the vertical drop below. In that stark flash, I saw not the valley floor but my daughter's bedroom in my house—the way it had looked that last night before everything changed.

"Every night in our old routine, like I'd done with Luke when he was younger, I'd tuck her in, whisper 'Daddy loves you' in her ear. Make sure she feels safe, pulling up her sheets." The memory tightened my chest. "Now some stranger does that. If anyone does at all."

Jonas was quiet for a long moment, letting the weather fill the silence. Finally, he said, "Tell me about that last night."

I closed my eyes against the bright sunlight reflecting from the rocks, letting the scene unfold.

---------------•●•---------------

The pale blue night shone behind Olivia's sheer curtains. Olivia sat cross-legged on her bed, Arnie curled up at her feet, as I closed the final box of her belongings. We'd both seen this day approaching. The joint custody situation wasn't working—for any of us. Olivia deserved stability, not the perpetual shuttling back and forth between houses, between parents who could no longer see eye to eye.

"Do I have to go, Dad?"

Her voice was small, uncertain—lost.

I set down the box and paused, choosing my words with care. We had both made choices that brought us to this moment: Dianne, by drawing the final curtain on a cohesive family life where custody was never Olivia's concern; and I, perhaps too rigid in my vision of what direction our family should take—what I thought was a New Zealand family.

"It's what's best for you, sweetheart," I said gently. "Being with your brother. Having one stable home."

The words tasted bitter, but they were true. The constant back-and-forth was wearing on both children. Luke had already chosen to stay primarily with his mother—whether out of comfort, convenience, or adolescent defiance didn't matter anymore. Olivia needed her mum and brother more than she needed to split her time evenly with me.

"But this is my home too."

That hurt. How many nights had we spent together in divorce, the two of us leading half a life each? Each night the same routine: pulling up her blankets, tucking her in, whispering "Daddy loves you," when she fell asleep. But love was not enough when it was fractured, served in weekly doses between two homes that could not find common ground.

I walked across to her bed and sat on the edge of it where I'd sat hundreds of times previously. "I know. And I'll still be your dad. That will never change." I made myself go on: "Your mum is trying her best, too, in her own way. We both want what's best for you and Luke."

It was real, even if I didn't agree with Dianne's approach. She made choices I found hard to understand—especially when it came to introducing Wayne to live with our children. I had asked to meet him, to have some sense of who was stepping into such a central part of their lives. That meeting never happened, and over time, my presence in the children's lives began to narrow in ways I hadn't expected.

I remember emailing Dianne about what Olivia needed by living with her full-time—stability, consistency, connection—and in her response, the focus seemed more on logistics and finances than the emotional wellbeing I was trying to express. At the time, it felt like compensation was being weighed more heavily than care. But as I stepped back, I began to see things differently.

Dianne was also trying to survive—rebuilding her identity and her future from the similar wreckage I was crawling through. It was the only way I could begin to make sense of her decisions without giving in to the raw, protective instincts that burned in me as a father.

Olivia embraced me, her tears dampening my shirt as we hugged.

A moment after finishing, Olivia said emphatically, "I don't want to go, Dad. I'm not leaving!" She cried as I hugged her tightly, catching the strawberry scent of her shampoo and struggling to keep embracing her.

The moment broke apart, breaking up into all the choices that brought us to this point:

The mid-week visits fell by the wayside when Luke withdrew, his sister eventually following along with him. The guarded space Dianne kept, shielding her new life as it kept me further away from the everyday lives of our children. My own withdrawal into work and projects, finding meaning in accomplishment when I should have been doing more to remain connected to them.

Olivia wouldn't leave by choice—how could she? Her concern was for me, not herself. Even at that youthful age, she worried about her father being without her. But watching her become increasingly isolated, missing time with school friends who all lived near her mother's house, I knew what had to be done. A father's love sometimes means making the hardest choice.

After our embrace and Olivia's defiance, she was not going to leave and, as I started loading her bags into the van, she tried to stop me. Her strong hands from all her years of horse riding grasped at the bag straps, trying to pull them back inside. My heart splintered, but I kept my voice gentle as I guided her from the front doorway.

"Come on sweetheart; we have to go." Each step felt like walking through deep water.

With her belongings in the van and Arnie already in the front, always quick to jump up into the van with an open door, she reluctantly stepped up into the front passenger seat.

The drive was wrapped in silence at first.

Then, a few kilometres from my house, I found the words…

"I know this isn't how either of us wanted this to happen. But no more juggling bags between houses, no more forgotten homework, sports gear, or horse-riding clothes." I glanced at her and caught her eyes. "This is better for you, even if it hurts right now."

"I know, Dad. I love you."

The words were quiet, resigned. Olivia no longer wanted to be at my home. She was tired of the shattered life and desired stability with her mum where socialising and friends were within reach. She knew I desired her happiness but didn't want to leave me behind. I could tell she comprehended the hurt of my custody falling to nothing.

We shared a final kiss goodbye after we both removed her bags from the van outside her mum's house.

It marked the end of my custody—from full-time care to shared time, and now, none. But this time, I had chosen it. I believed Olivia's future, her wellbeing, required stability—more than my part-time presence could offer.

Driving away that afternoon, leaving her to live with her mother and someone I'd never had the opportunity to meet, felt like something in me was being torn from the inside. I kept driving—faster than I should have—because some part of me feared that if I slowed, I'd return. Claiming my daughter away from the unwelcome world I'd just released her into.

For two months, I didn't hear from Olivia. I left messages and voice notes—gentle reminders that she hadn't been abandoned. That I had made this choice out of love, not distance. I wanted her to know I still saw her, still held her in my heart, even if I wasn't part of her daily life anymore. I understood that things had changed, that her phone and contact were now part of a different rhythm—one I was no longer part of.

Then, on Father's Day, I received a call from Child Services. They had questions— concerns—about how I'd handled Olivia's final handover. It felt like a final blow. I'd made what I believed was the best decision for her—and now, the way I'd shown my loving insistence was being questioned by some random employee of the State.

I believe Olivia understood, even then. That day was hard for her too, leaving my care, watching everything change. I imagine she cried uncontrollably when she got home. Why wouldn't she? It was the end of something familiar. But the report didn't come from her voice. It was someone else's interpretation of the moment— someone watching from the outside.

That call hurt more than I can say—not just because it came on Father's Day, but because it framed love and grief as something to be feared.

But those months of silence were their own kind of penance.

I thought about how, four years before this, I spotted them from my car—Dianne, Luke, Olivia, and Wayne cycling together along the river path. Their wheels turned in synchronisation, seeing them in unison through my open window. Luke led the group; my children being followed by their now male unchosen leader accepting his role as naturally supported by the kid's mother. The vision pushed me toward a rage followed by a depression unable to digest the shock and loss of what was once mine but also forced me to confront reality: my kids' lives would move forward with or without my daily involvement. I could adapt to this new normal or risk losing them completely.

I started to slowly try and reconstruct myself soon after that. Not for revenge or pity, but survival. For the chance to be what type of father they still could use, even if it wasn't the one I had wanted to be. The father who could let go of his own expectations and accept the reduced role he was dealt, hoping that someday the gap might open again.

The most demanding thing I learned was not how to survive without the everyday moments—the bedtime stories, the morning kisses, the middle-of-the-night 'I love yous'. It was accepting that sometimes loving means moving backward, allowing your children to forge their own way, even if it's away from you. It was having faith that the foundation you've built will be sufficient to draw them back in when they're ready.

I used her brightly-coloured phone charging cable years after she left it behind at my house—not as a grasp on what was gone but as a reminder that love evolves just the way the colours changed charging my phone. It morphs to accommodate new situations, becoming more powerful by changing.

Morning sunlight streaming through her bare window created shadows where her bed stood. Yet they were no sounds of Olivia —just signs of transition. A made bed, a few unwanted posters and photos left behind on the wall. Visible history of the gap between what was and what could yet be. I hoped that if I were courageous enough to continue growing, continue loving without insisting, trust that time and truth would find their own path forward.

---•●•---

A wind squall hit me as I hauled myself back from the recollection. Bright sun rays lashed against the granite between the clouds, highlighting some holds. My boots grated on still damp rock as Jonas balanced on a thin ledge just above.

"Your heart made it, anyway," he shouted looking down at me, as the wind tried to soften his voice. Sweat drops running down his weathered face.

Our path became narrower, requiring absolute concentration. Gravel shattered under every careful step. The lake disappeared far below in the distance under veils of light sent between the clouds, the valley obscured below.

"Part of it died that day," I snarled, reaching for a solid grip. "The part that believed I could protect them from every hurt. Keep their world perfect." My hand closed on a sharp granite hold. "The rest of it had to harden up."

Jonas gestured ahead, pointing toward a safer path. The wind screamed between us, attempting to tear us from the cliff face. "Like this mountain—naked rock but standing."

As we hauled ourselves upwards, the sun burst through the grey clouds intermittently, lighting the natural patterns in the rock. It was beautiful, even though it was shattered, even though it was scarred. It was strong.

"You want to hear the strangest thing?" my voice rode barely above the wind. "All those years, I worked to give them the perfect life, the whole family I never had. And then one text message, and it all fell apart anyway." I laughed bitterly. "Now here I am, back where my heart was left behind fifteen years ago. Full circle."

"Maybe that's the plan," Jonas said. His boots loosening scree scuttering down just missing me as he ascended higher. "Coming back not to reclaim what's lost, but to find out what's still possible."

The rocky path merged with the ridge up ahead rougher than ever, yet firm. Real. A path forward, though not the one I'd planned.

My legs hurt as we trekked the final couple of meters up to the jacked rock ledge. It was still windy but less so. Gaps in the clouds provided views of the blue sky above.

"You know what I learned?" I stopped to breathe, gazing up at the summit. "You can go ahead and construct the perfect shelter, battle every storm. But sometimes." I swept my arm out at the stark beauty surrounding us. "Sometimes you must learn to stand exposed."

Jonas nodded, comprehension in his eyes. Eyes that looked strangely familiar in the fading light.

The path unwound before me, disappearing to leave my judgment on which ascent to take. Peering ahead looking up for a safe passage. But for the first time on this ascent, I approached peace. Not as though I'd received all the answers, but since I'd ceased anticipating that they would arrive in the form I desired.

You must let the mountain guide you the way sometimes, even if the way up seems impassable. Even if it is about growing stronger from what shatters you.

The only real challenge is not the summit—it's continuing to climb when the path disappears. When all that remains is faith in your resilience to adapt, persevere, and move forward one step at a time.

Thunder boomed in the distance threatening to unleash its full fury as we slung our packs over our shoulders.

The storm's worst had moved past us only threatening us with what dangers could have ensured had we been in its direct path. I felt the mountain had spared us the dire consequences of her full fury happening only kms away. I wondered if she was listening to me during the ascent. Sparing me to what storms had already been endured in another world back home. The air felt crisp and clean.

I felt ready for what lay ahead.

4

ECHOES OF YOUTH

Childhood memories and their influence on fatherhood

A high cloud passed overhead, briefly dimming the sunlight as we picked our way across the broken trail. Jonas moved with the easy confidence of someone intimately familiar with the mountain, finding solid footholds where I saw only loose scree and treacherous drops.

"Tell me about those first nights of separation," Jonas said, pausing to adjust the frayed straps of his pack. Sunlight, catching the worn canvas, highlighting patches that had been mended and re-mended. "After the text."

My throat constricted at the recollection. "I spent the first night in my company's training room. My business, one that I'd built from the ground up, was my refuge." I sniggered. "No shower there—had to purchase a rubber hose at the hardware store, rig it up in the men's bathroom. Ice-water cold, years-thick grimy tiles. But I could not go back to my house."

"Pride?" Jonas questioned.

"Survival." The word tasted sharp on my tongue. "I knew if I stayed, there'd be a fight. And my kids would be watching. Also, I was told that all it takes is a loud word spoken or interpreted as said, and a restraining order can be applied and then issued from the Family Court that would make it impossible to ever come back to the family home. To my kids. The implications were far greater with a possible court application preventing me from ever having shared custody of kids. That would have been no different than being executed. And what would the kids think of their dad then, not being able to be with them? This manufactured situation was hard enough, so I stayed away to gather my thoughts. I was absent for only a few nights and then returned home on the advice from my lawyer not to leave the family home or 'abandonment' can also be brought against me. I was living in an actual hell."

Jonas nodded, understanding darkening his eyes. Wind whipped his jacket, snapping the fabric like a flag of surrender.

"She wanted me to leave first," I told Jonas quietly. "She grew more impatient as the weeks went by. 'When are you moving out? This has gone on long enough,' she'd say."

I remember the rage that simmered just beneath the surface—still do. But when I finally spoke, it came out calm, steady. "I've done nothing wrong."

I had given everything I could: a beautiful home, travel memories, financial security, the ability for Dianne to be a full-time mother—something I'd supported wholeheartedly. I saw myself as a present father, a loyal partner, a husband who worked hard but made lots of time for his family. And yet, there I was—facing the reality of leaving the life I'd helped build. Being asked to pack a bag and walk away from my children, from the home that had been born of my efforts and dreams.

The air became cooler as we ascended, with each breath becoming more difficult as we reached higher altitudes. The lake shone far beneath with patches of darkness where the wind gusts had hit the surface under sparse clouds.

"I refused," I said, my voice steady but heavy. "Told her if she wanted the separation, she could be the one to leave. And she did. Packed her things that night and drove off. It wasn't without a final plea—I held her, promising we could start over and fix whatever had come between us. But she stiffened at my touch, her reluctance unmistakable. With a resolute 'no,' she loosened my grip, picked up her overnight bag, walked to the garage, and drove away."

I shook my head, gathering my thoughts before continuing. "That was it. I realized then—there was no undoing the wreckage of my family. The finality settled over me, but beneath the weight of loss, I felt a sliver of power, grateful for my lawyer's advice in what had become a losing game. I was at home with my kids."

I paused, the memory lingering, then continued, my gaze distant. "I stood in the driveway, watching her car taillights disappear, knowing everything had changed forever."

Jonas studied me, his eyes sharp, that unsettling intensity growing familiar. "The children?" he asked.

"Asleep in their rooms," I replied quietly. "Innocent. They had no idea their world was shattered."

I swallowed hard, the lump in my throat thickening. "I went into Luke and Olivia's rooms after Dianne left, kissing them goodnight like always did. But it was... hollow. Everything felt wrong. Like I was already a ghost in my own house."

Thunder rumbled from the peaks adjacent to us. Jonas tilted his head, measuring the storm's distance. "What happened next?"

"The dance began. One week with me, one week with her. Every Sunday at four, I would watch them load their backpacks into her car. It was like dying all over again each time." I kicked a loose rock and watched it scatter off into space. "But

I had to be steady. Kids are always watching, taking note of every reaction. They become the most important judges."

"Did you bury your feelings?"

"Had to. Or at least tried to. For them." The wind carried murmurs of possible rain. "But that's when I knew I needed help. You can't get through that kind of pain by yourself. Saw a counsellor, started working through it. Had to find my footing before I could attempt to help them find theirs."

We came to a narrow shelf cut into the mountain side. The valley floor below was impossibly far away. Dark clouds massed above, threatening even worse weather we thought had slipped by relieving us of its intensity.

"The toughest thing wasn't the logistics," I said, testing each step before transferring my weight. "It was holding onto dignity when everything in you wants to scream. To finally speak the things, you've kept quiet—the confusion around that first text, the scripted language that felt rehearsed, not real. You wonder who said what, who suggested which words, and why it all sounded so final."

I paused, swallowing the emotion. "It's learning to smile when you know she's out with friends and the kids are asking, 'Why isn't Mummy coming home tonight?' And it's holding your tongue when all you want is to say how you really feel—but you don't. Because little ears are always listening."

Jonas tensed as a blast of wind tried to rip us from our tenuous hold. "I am not afraid of the truth."

"You do what you have to. For them." I squinted up at the threatening sky. "But first you have to find a reason to keep going. A purpose bigger than the pain."

Lightning split the clouds, illuminating the path we still had to climb. Jonas waited, letting the thunder fade before asking: "Did you find one?"

I smiled, though it held more shadows than light. "I was about to. But that's another story."

Heavy drops of rain began to strike the rocks around us as we pressed on, seeking shelter from the gathering storm. Yet somehow, each step felt surer than the last—as if by revisiting these wounds, I was finally learning to carry their weight.

We found shelter beneath an overhanging rock as the rain quickly intensified. Water streamed down the cliff face, turning the granite dark. Jonas shrugged off his pack, settling onto a relatively dry patch of scree.

"Tell me about the counselling," he said, pulling out a battered water bottle. "What made you decide to go?"

I watched sheets of rain sweep across the valley below. "Childhood ghosts, mostly. I'd seen what divorce did to kids—lived it myself at sixteen. Knew I needed tools to help myself navigate what had arrived, knowing there was more coming."

"What did you learn?"

"That survival means different things to different people." I accepted the water bottle he offered, took a long drink. "Dianne's version meant nights out, social circles, and building a new life separate from the old. Mine meant finding stability in the chaos—still running my business and financially providing for her and the kids, being the steady presence our kids needed. Not running away."

Thunder cracked overhead, the sound reverberating off stone. Jonas waited for it to fade before speaking. "Must have been hard, watching her move on while you were still processing."

"It was like watching a performance from backstage—seeing all the mechanisms that created the illusion." I handed the water bottle back. "Her friends supported her choices, celebrating her new chapter with enthusiasm. I'm sure they meant well, but from where I stood, it was hard to watch. At school pickups, I'd overhear stories of big nights out—supportive mums rallying around her as she embraced her independence."

I exhaled, my voice softening. "Meanwhile, I was at home, trying to answer Luke and Olivia's questions. Why Mum wasn't home for dinner. Why things felt different."

"You sound angry."

"Not anymore," I said, leaning against the cold stone. "But at the time? Rage. Humiliation. Confusion. The counsellor helped me see it for what it was. That I had to redirect all that energy—use it for something constructive, or let it consume everything."

Jonas regarded me with those strangely recognizable eyes. "Like what?"

"I had started creating an app and continued with it tirelessly, if you can imagine. Something to help people who experience anxiety and depression." I had a hint of a smile on my face. "Ironic, I know—creating tools to combat mental health issues while grappling with my own demons. But it gave me an enormous and important purpose when I needed it most."

The rain started to stop, although menacing clouds continued to hover overhead. A single ray of sunlight broke through, illuminating the lake far beneath and throwing its surface into liquid silver.

"The counsellor told me one thing that I remember," I went on. "Told me that sometimes we have to release the form we'd envisioned our lives would take. That change isn't failure."

"Did you think that?"

"Not initially. Kept believing if I only worked harder, made cleverer choices, I could turn it all around." I saw another sunbeam spear through the heavy clouds. "But you can't keep someone who's already gone in their heart. You can only control how you respond to what's next."

Jonas nodded slowly. "For the kids."

"Always for the children. Every choice, every response, every word we say or don't say—they're watching, learning to navigate life's toughest moments by the way we navigate ours. So, I couldn't just lie down and die, though there were moments when I wished I could. They needed to know you could survive tragedy with integrity or at least see me trying. That pain doesn't necessarily make you bitter."

"Even when it hurts?"

"Especially then." I rose to my feet, trying the weather. The rain had let up, but the path in front of me shone continuously wet. "That's what the counselling instilled in me—pain is unavoidable, but suffering is a choice. You can allow it to shatter you or harness it as fuel to make yourself something better. Applying this wisdom was challenging, as rage often surged in response to the frequent triggers of pain."

Jonas shrugged his pack on, ready to go on. "And which did you choose?" The question hung suspended in the heavy moist air between us. Down below, patches of sunlight moved across the valley floor, banishing shadows. Up above, the storm was breaking up, and patches of blue sky were visible through the clouds. "I opted to climb, which also meant falling down many times. That's what happens when you climb, you also slip. It's unavoidable," I said at last. "Even when the summit was out of view. Even when each step pained me."

"Because sometimes the sole direction is upward." We stepped out of our refuge into the storm's aftermath. The air of the mountains was again fresh and revitalized. Every breath tasted like promise. "Besides," I continued along the path, "I had a promise to keep. "To whom?" Jonas questioned.

But I didn't respond. Just kept walking, step by step, as the memories of a younger, less experienced me wrapped around the edges of my thoughts like mountain mist.

---•●•---

I received a Father's Day card from Luke a few years after separation. His message was a testament that the kids are always watching.

Luke's card really moved me, with each word selected with care. His recognition of my perseverance—and more so, that he had witnessed me struggle on but not shatter—was proof that in all the chaos, I had succeeded in demonstrating to him something worthwhile about enduring challenges. The visual depictions of automobiles, the mountain bike, and windsurfing boards symbolized the activities he knew were my passions and could potentially enjoy again. In those mere drawings and genuine words was proof that our bond, though strained and altered, still existed.

The path narrowed as we climbed higher, forcing at best a single file. Jonas led the way, his boots finding purchase on wet stone with uncanny certainty. The wind had died, and clouds now clung to the mountainside, transforming familiar landmarks into ghostly shapes.

"You spoke of a promise," he said across his shoulder. "Of what kind?"

I collected myself before responding. "It began with a photograph. Discovered it while taking some personal items from home to the warehouse office during that first week—me at age six, smiling at the camera as if I held all of life's secrets." The recollection choked me. "That boy was so full of hope, so sure good things were on the horizon. Looking at him, I knew I couldn't disappoint him."

---•●•---

The light in the business's storeroom flickered as I rummaged through dusty files looking for my personal items kept over the years, dust particles dancing in the faint fluorescent light. My bed, a roll-out mat I purchased with the shower hose, was rolled up in the corner out of the training room behind a display stand so not to publicise my family collapse to the business's loyal customers. The rubber hose used to shower lay coiled beside it like a dead snake.

Two days now since I'd received the message. Two nights of scrubbing up in icy water, sleeping on cold floors where I had delivered my devastating news to my staff. The showroom continued to gleam with its usual precision, but here, in my temporary haven, things were unravelling.

With no sign of the few items I was looking for, I went home during a time I knew the house would be empty. No ex-wife, Luke or Olivia. When I arrived and entered, I felt a coldness like a vacuum had sucked the optimism and life from the once-family home. I was there to grieve and return my personal belongings to the business. A place of sanctuary where keepsake items would be secure. I went into my home office upstairs and opened a cabinet which held some envelopes of photos that were passed on to me when my father died and then my mother. I fumbled through a few large brown envelopes when a beige manila envelope stood out. My name was scrawled across it in my mother's script handwriting—one of the few things I wanted when she'd died.

My hands shook while I was opening it. Out spilled photographs—pieces of a childhood I vividly remembered. There I was at age three, holding a toy truck. At five, with missing front teeth. And then—

The picture stole my breath. Age six, in my grandparent's backyard. Standing beside my two-and-a-half-meter timber tower I had just made under my grandfather's house in his workshop. Summer sun caught in my hair; eyes squinted against the sun. But the smile really got me—huge, unguarded, utterly convinced that life had only good things ahead. No idea that in the coming years my family would shatter. That I'd lose friends to addiction, watch my father die too young, feel my mother's rejection like a stab to the heart in my twenties and see her later passing of Motor Neurone Disease.

I fell to the floor, weak in the knees. The slate floor was cold under my dress pants, but I barely noticed. That boy's face had me under a spell—his innocence, his hope, his pure heart that hadn't yet learned to fear.

"I'm sorry," I whispered, my hand on the gleaming surface. Sorry for letting life dull that shine. I'm so sorry for failing. Sorry for not looking after you better. Sorry for ending up broken, sleeping on warehouse floors while my children's lives fell apart.

But as I gazed at that younger version of myself, tears streaming and dripping onto the matte photo paper, something in my chest realigned. This boy deserved better than sacrificing. He deserved better than the life he'd found now. Looking at his face told me of far greater expectations.

"I won't let you down," I vowed to him, holding the photo up close. "No matter what, I'll figure out a way through this. For you. For Luke and Olivia. I'll teach them how to live with honour. I will not let life break you too, young Mark. You deserve a wonderful life. This will not be the end for you. Your survival and peace will be my mission." Goosebumps penetrated my body as I wiped my flowing tears away. This was a promise to my young self. No one on this earth could force me to break this and certainly not my ex-wife Dianne.

I drove slowly back to the business allowing my swollen face to rescind. Sitting back at my office I stared at the photo and felt a warmth of fond memories carrying the tower out of the workshop and under the balcony where I climbed up and peered over the edge to see my parents and grandparents playing cards. I remember Dad staring in shock, unknowingly holding his cards up for all to see, watching my smile peering at both my grandparents, my mum, and him from over the balcony.

From my office I could hear my staff talking to customers, the phones ringing and trucks unloading. It was business as usual. But in my mind, my focus was different.

I slid the picture cautiously into my wallet, alongside photos of my kids. A reminder of the person I once was—and could be again, if only I were courageous enough.

Jonas stopped at a switchback, waiting for me to catch up with him. "Tell me more."

"That photo saved my life more than once," I told Jonas, coming back to the present. The mountain air was drying my lungs. "When things got darkest, I'd look at it and remember my promise. Remember that I had to keep climbing, if only to do right by that boy, young innocent Mark."

Jonas gazed at me with those discomfortingly knowing eyes. "Sounds like he was your compass."

"My motivation to keep climbing and stay alive, yeah." I strapped my pack over my shoulder, preparing to depart. "Oddly enough, working on my mental health app I invented, I realized that's what I was trying to create—a way for people to send messages of encouragement, break up bad thought patterns. Exactly what that photo did for me."

"Life has a way of coming full circle."

"Sometimes quite literally." I motioned out toward the mountain that surrounded us. "Fifteen years ago, I was surrounded by these slopes with dreams of the future. Now here I am, talking to that same young heart, attempting to map my way forward again."

Jonas smiled—that same unsettling smile that always gave me pause for a second. "Perhaps that's why you're here. Not to get back what you've lost, but to recall who you were before the world began to break and teach you to fear."

I looked at him more closely then, something nagging at the fringes of perception. But whenever I would grasp it, he was already in motion once more, ascending.

The trail angled sharply upward. It was even more precarious than before, and every step demanded complete focus, with no space for memory or sorrow. And yet somehow, I was lighter than I had been before, as if by telling these burdens, I was learning to hold them differently.

"Do you know what the most difficult lesson was?" I yelled up to Jonas. "To learn that sometimes the best way to stay true to your younger self is to let go of the life you imagined. Accept that evolving means changing, even when it hurts."

He stopped, turned around to face me. Sunlight caught his profile at precisely the right angle for a brief moment, and I could have sworn—

But clouds passed, shadows returned, and he was just another hiker again. "Ready to head back down?" he asked.

I shifted my pack straps, sensing the electricity in the air. There was another storm brewing somewhere over the summits, but I was not afraid this time. Sometimes you must walk in the rain to get home.

"Yep, ready. I've hit my max today," I answered, looking cautiously over the ledge and between the clouds below where the valley hosted farmlands in miniature scale. From that rocky ridge, we began our careful descent. The undulated rocky trail demanded as much attention going down as it had coming up. The craggy path we'd climbed with such effort now stretched with gaps of emptiness in between, guiding us, requiring our own contributions to find our way back to where we'd begun—though I was no longer the same man who had started this journey.

5

THE WAY THINGS WERE

Remembering family life before the breakdown

By the time Jonas and I reached the carpark at the conclusion of our initial day of hiking, the sun had broken the darkest clouds and was starting to set below jagged peaks. They were capped in soft white wispy effects surrounding us and all the mountains to the horizon. Golden light slanted through the large, craggy rocks, sending shafts of light and dappled shade onto the trails end at our feet.

"Big day," Jonas said, lifting his pack further up onto his shoulder. His voice had a contented sound, as though he had discovered what he was looking for on the trail.

"That's an understatement," I commiserated, shifting the burden of my own pack with every step. The physical fatigue was nothing compared to the emotional toll of reliving some of the worst experiences of my life. Yet there was a strange lightness to it as well, as though by releasing the words out into the air, I'd lost some of their hold on me.

We made it to the car, and I rummaged around for my keys, my fingers shaking with exhaustion, most of my food supplies left untouched. Hunger forgotten with the intensity of thoughts both up and down the mountain. Jonas propped himself against the hood, his eyes far away as he stared out across the valley below.

"You know," he continued after a pause, "I envy you in a sense."

I stopped, the key half-way in the lock. "Envy me? Why?"

Jonas shrugged, a bitter smile twisting his lips. "You've lived, Mark. Lived, I mean. You've loved, lost, and experienced things that most people can't even dream of." He shook his head, awe and pity combining on his face. "That sort of pain, it does something to you. Breaks you open, but perhaps that's the only way to allow the light in."

I stared at him, struggling to align this wisdom with the carefree hiker I had just met. "Jonas, I. I don't know what to say."

He stepped back from the car, adjusting his pack. "You don't have to say anything. Just keep moving, yeah? Keep climbing, even when you can't see the summit." His presence was reassuring, warm and steady. "Because I swear to you, the view at the top? It's worth every step."

With that, he turned around and walked down the path that led out of the car park. I blinked, a question forming on my lips as I opened my phone curious to see the photos I'd captured.

"Wait, don't you have a ride? Where are you going to stay?"

But when I looked again, the path was empty. Jonas was nowhere to be found.

Apprehension tickled the nape of my neck as I climbed into the car and turned the key in the ignition. Jonas's words replayed in my mind as I drove down from the mountain carpark, the shadows growing darker with every turn in the road.

Keep climbing.

But for what was I climbing? The life I knew was gone from me, shattered like the illusions I had cherished so long and so tenaciously. And the future. Well, that was as vague and shapeless as the mist now settling on the valley floor below.

I started driving back to the hotel for the night, my legs throbbing from the day's hike but my head spinning from the topics Jonas and I had discussed on the trail. Cruising through the dwindling landscape, memories of happier times before the breakup started rising to the surface, as real as the day they occurred.

----------•●•----------

I remembered our trip to Switzerland when Luke was eight and Olivia just four. Staying in Lucerne and riding the luge at Mt Pilatus—those weeks were a tapestry of moments I'd later cling to during the darkest days of our separation. We'd spent weeks exploring Europe, Dianne meticulously planning each day like she did with everything.

In Naples, Luke had been fascinated by the ancient architecture, his young mind absorbing every detail about historical sites. Luke with his cool head of blonde hair and inquiring blue eyes, always analysing things with fierce focus—the same face he had when we constructed remote control cars in the garage or when he rode his first bicycle with me holding him up, his little body in a red helmet tilting forward in determination.

Struggling with low muscle tone, Olivia would carefully hold my hand as we navigated cobblestone streets, her determination shining brighter than her physical challenges. Her long blond curly hair gleaming in the sunlight as she skipped a few steps alongside me, usually in her favourite pink dresses, her face illuminating with the same bright smile that would meet me years later when we'd cook together in the kitchen, her joyous expression as she made her favourite treat of caramel slice during our cherished weeks together.

One evening in a small Tuscan village, we'd sat at an outdoor café—the kind of place we'd dreamed about during our early years of marriage. Luke was sketching the street scene in a notebook I'd bought him, his tongue stuck out in concentration. Olivia played with her pasta, creating elaborate designs that made Dianne laugh— that laugh I'd fallen in love with years ago. The golden light had caught Dianne's hair, and for a moment, everything felt perfect. We were a tight unit then: four people bound by love, possibility, and shared dreams of a simpler quality of life beyond Perth's mining boom mentality.

I'd looked at Dianne and thought this is what we promised each other. This moment of pure, uncomplicated joy—before the business consumed me, before her social nights out began to replace our family movies, before we forgot how to find our way back to each other.

———————————·●·———————————

Three years before Dianne sent that fateful text, she and I were sitting in a trendy café, lattes steaming between us as we pored over a stack of glossy school brochures. Luke was still a few years away from needing placement, but we wanted to be proactive. With her researching mind and my business acumen, we made a formidable team when we were on the same page.

"What about this one?" Dianne tapped a perfectly manicured nail against a photograph of smiling students in crisp uniforms. "They have an excellent sports program and student support programs."

I flipped to the tuition page, my eyebrows lifting at the numbers. "And an excellent way of providing the best for our kids," I nodded appreciatively. Dianne was always thorough with her school research, finding options I wouldn't have considered.

Dianne rolled her eyes, but there was no heat behind it. "Don't be dramatic. You know we can afford it."

She was right, of course. My business was thriving—had been for years now. We'd gone from struggling to make ends meet to having more money than we knew what to do with. But old memories of struggling as a young adult die hard, and a part of me still worried the bottom would fall out any day. I remember one of the best meals I had was when I was 18 years old, after finding a two-dollar coin cleaning my car. Just enough to buy half-price chicken and chips for dinner. So different from the extravagant meals of our current life.

"I just want to make sure we're making the right choice," I said, reaching across the table to take her hand. "For both of them. Especially Olivia. I know Luke will thrive anywhere."

Dianne's expression softened at the mention of our daughter. Olivia's early challenges in her development took us by surprise. Dianne, determined to give her every advantage, was particularly wonderful with Olivia back then—her patience and dedication to researching every possible therapy and support system showed what an amazing mother she was, especially when it came to navigating Olivia's unique needs. Luke was more resilient, excelling at whatever consumed his interest, so adaptability wasn't for him such an issue.

"Of course," Dianne agreed, lacing her fingers through mine. "Only the best for our kids."

The waiter then appeared, refilling our cups and whisking away our plates. As he moved off, I found myself studying Dianne's face in the warm afternoon light filtering through the café windows. She was as beautiful as the day I'd met her all those years ago.

But in that moment, after discussing school situations and knowing a place for our son was unlikely due to an unexpected demand from overseas mining migrants clogging the placements of the best schools in Perth, there was a weariness around her eyes that hadn't been there before, a restlessness in the way her gaze flitted around the room.

I pushed down a flicker of unease, chalking it up to the stress of the school search and the never-ending demands of raising two children while running a household and supporting me in my growing business. We'd get through this, just like we'd weathered every other challenge that had come our way. Together.

Just a few years before everything fell apart, we'd spent entire weekends together. Some days in the hills and some riding around the river in Perth. I'd invested in bikes for everyone—Luke's was a specialized junior racing model he'd selected after his research. The number of gears and type of brakes essential. Olivia's a carefully adapted bike that would attach to mine, allowing her to ride and relax during our cycling journeys. We'd pack snacks for our rides, Dianne creating those with balanced nutrition and the kids' favourite treats.

Those biking adventures were our sanctuary. Luke would race ahead, jumping curbs between parked cars, his adventurous spirit already evident, while I called out technical instructions about gear shifting and sometimes trail navigation in the hills. Olivia would be in a specially designed bike trailer, her laugh cutting through the morning stillness. Sometimes Arnie the dog would run alongside, tongue lolling, a small furry guardian of our family unit. We'd stop along the river, share water bottles, take family selfies that never quite captured how we felt in those moments.

These weren't just bike rides. They were our weekly recommitment to the family we'd built, the dreams we'd shared when we first married—before the business demands, my susceptibility to stress, and Dianne's social nights out and increasing distance from me, before we started living parallel lives under the same roof.

———————————•●•———————————

Years before that, our Sunday mornings had been sacred. Dianne would wake before anyone, carefully preparing pancakes from a recipe her mother had taught her. I'd wake up to put on music—a mix of pop and indie tracks we'd discovered during our early dating years—and the kids would shortly rise to dance in their pyjamas between the kitchen and living room. Luke would attempt to help, more determined than skilled, sending flour and batter flying. Olivia would be right beside him, sometimes with me helping her make movements to the music beats from her soft limbs, each a careful negotiation, but her spirit unbroken.

This was our family's liturgy—a reminder of why we'd chosen each other, why we'd built this life. Luke would recount stories from his week, Olivia would show us her latest art project, and Dianne and I would exchange those private looks that spoke volumes about our connection. In those moments, our family felt like a perfectly calibrated machine: each part moving in harmony, supporting the others, believing totally in our collective potential.

I didn't know then how fragile that harmony was, how easily it could be dismantled by work stress, unspoken resentments, or the slow drift that happens when two people stop truly seeing each other.

———————————•●•———————————

The rental car's headlights cut through the gathering dusk, illuminating the narrow road winding down to the hotel. I leaned back in my seat, letting my mind drift to eleven years before, when Dianne and I holidayed in New Zealand. A subsequent trip four years after first falling in love with the country and lifestyle it offered during a holiday in Queenstown.

It was meant to be a relaxing getaway, and a chance to reconnect away from the grind of daily life. The trip also had another intention: to discover whether New Zealand could host our future one last time. I was driving this cause with Dianne following somewhat subdued. And for a while, it was a reconnection until that became unstuck after we'd marvelled at the breathtaking vistas, soaked in natural hot springs, and gorged ourselves on fresh seafood and local wine.

As we walked on stunning trails and drove through quaint towns, Dianne and I began to talk about a different kind of future one last time. Four years after the first attempt to consider New Zealand home failed. The attraction of a simple life and one away from the materialism and egos that seemed to be taking over Perth resurfaced with conviction from me. One where we could raise our children in a place that valued community, nature and connection over social status and wealth.

"Can you imagine living here?" I whispered to her, my voice thick with uncertainty. "Waking up to this every day?" I had asked this question four years prior with a hint of possibility. I was both optimistically and ignorantly looking for a reply of conviction. To agree on our family's new future.

She sighed, shaking her head. "It's not right for us, Mark." Not enough for Olivia, not enough for me, leaving out Luke who she knew was made for the steep trails and who would fit into the mountain life like a clove. "We need to go back."

I felt the desperation claw at my throat. "But this is our last chance, don't you see? Our last chance to give the kids the childhood we always wanted for them. To prioritize family over the endless cycle of more, more, more."

I couldn't understand why she was resisting. I had been to the same school appointments as Dianne in this growing New Zealand mountain town and at first, we both felt optimistic. So why had Dianne changed? Was it because I'd suggested buying a business in Sydney, transitioning between our mountain village home for a while to secure financial stability? I knew that was the right move.

I wondered aloud. "I'm right about that, aren't I? Why's it so hard to see?"

Her response was cold, sharp. "It's my turn to do what I want, Mark. I've followed your plans long enough."

I wasn't backing down. "Fine," I said, "If you can replace the provision I make for the family, no problem."

But there was no response. Just a defiant, unwavering "no," despite the life we could have had.

And so, we went back. Back to the life I'd thought we were escaping, the one I could feel closing in around me. One I'd outgrown.

We returned to our responsibilities and routines. My business was a cash machine churning out profits, but had stopped growing. My interest faded without the dream of paradise in NZ for my family. I'd 'lived' the Perth life and was unmotivated past my App. We had bought a beautiful home in an affluent suburb by the Swan River, the kind of place I'd once dreamed of providing for my family, but now 4726 km from ideal. It was surrounded by mansions all with high fences offering an absent community feel. See no one, hear no one. No kids riding around. A wealthy place, but so cold.

---•●•---

Now, in the quiet stillness of the rental car, I was reminded of what I realised when our Perth Mansion was purchased instead of a property in the New Zealand mountain town. It was simply a double-story modern rendered cage trapping us in a life void of optimism.

I pulled into the hotel car park, Dianne's words echoing in my head as I climbed out of the car. "There's just not enough here for Olivia or me."

The previous day, watching young children playing around the nearby lake and riding horses in paddocks on the village outskirts reminded me of how much I used to disagree with Dianne a decade ago. Watching teenage boys riding their mountain bikes, dirty from having just finished riding world-class downhill trails. Even mums were joyous outside the cafes with young kids hovering around in dirty clothes suited for exploring the surrounding paddocks and hills closer to the town. Here was all that I wished for our children.

It had been the final blow, shattering the fragile hope I'd been nurturing that we could make a fresh start at the time.

In the hotel room, I collapsed onto the bed, staring up at the ceiling as if it held the answers I'd spent the last decade searching for. When had it all started to unravel? Was there a moment I could have changed course, made a different choice that would have kept our family from splintering apart?

———————— ·●· ————————

My thoughts returned to that Monday morning, standing by the post box, holding the prestigious Perth secondary school acceptance envelope for Luke's Year 7 placement. Finally, a yes—after months of uncertainty and an earlier, disheartening no.

At the time, Perth's elite schools were overflowing, with many spots taken by families relocating for the booming mining sector—professionals brought in from around the world to meet the state's rapid growth. We had already sold our Perth home and made plans to relocate to New Zealand, when Dianne—at the eleventh hour—said no. I proposed Melbourne instead, the city where we had both grown up. A place that felt familiar, stable, and full of possibility.

Eager for a fresh start, we purchased a home in Melbourne while our container of belongings still sat in a freight depot back in Perth. But then came the twist: the school acceptance for Luke arrived out of nowhere that Monday morning. Just like that, Perth became the default. New Zealand faded. So did Melbourne.

On the advice of a particularly good lawyer, I pulled out of the Melbourne house purchase before settlement. All that remained were the pieces of a broken dream— what I had believed was right for our family.

Still, I buried the disappointment. Suppressed the whisper of doubt that told me Perth wasn't the future I had envisioned. I drowned it in the flurry of false relief that came with the school letter, and the tasks of settling into yet another new home. I returned to the role I knew well: provider, breadwinner, the one who kept everything moving forward but this time in a place I felt was no longer my 'right' home.

But something else was shifting beneath the surface. Dianne was drifting further away. I could feel it—though we didn't speak of it directly. More nights out with friends. Weekends filled with social plans. Less time at the dinner table or on the couch for movie nights. Fewer slow Sundays in pyjamas with the kids, fewer bike rides and pancake mornings. We were still under one roof, but the sense of family we once built together had started to thin like mist in the morning sun.

—————————•●•—————————

I squeezed my eyes shut against the sting of tears, grief and regret, a hard knot in my throat. I'd seen the signs but hadn't wanted to believe what they meant. Those years ago, I hadn't wanted to face the fact that the woman I loved was pulling away, that the vision of the future we'd once shared was crumbling before my eyes.

Sleep was a long time coming that night, the ghosts of the past crowding close in the unfamiliar room. But as I finally drifted off, it was with a grim sort of clarity, the knowledge that I couldn't change what had already happened settling like a weight in my chest.

All I could do was keep moving forward, one step at a time, for my distant children and for the man I still hoped to become. At least at this moment, I was in NZ to contemplate the future of my life. Now, a lonely, once hands-on father, feeling somewhat broken without purpose.

And for that bright-eyed six-year-old boy I'd once been, the one who still believed in happily ever after, no matter how unlikely it seemed.

I owed it to him to try.

6

LOVE YOUR BODY

Reclaiming physical strength and letting go of dependencies

Dawn broke cold and clear over the mountain town. The night's rain had washed the world clean, leaving behind a bright sky and air so pure it seemed almost medicinal. I stood at my hotel window, watching early light crawl across the jagged peaks, revealing contours hidden yesterday by cloud and mist.

My stiffen muscles ached from the previous day's climb, but beneath the soreness lay something else—a subdued readiness to go on. Not only back up the mountain, but into the memories I'd kept hidden for so long. There was meaning in this climb now—questions I needed to ask, not only for me, but for that six-year-old boy in the picture who was owed the life I'd promised him.

The mountain would be waiting. I grabbed my pack and headed out.

The trailhead parking lot held only three other vehicles when I arrived. The solitude suited me. I checked my supplies hardly touched from the day before, needing only to add a bottle of water and protein bar, laced my boots tight, and looked up at the trail ahead. I checked my passport was in the top pouch of my pack, the same as the day before. Just in case things didn't work out on the mountain. Yesterday's rain had carved fresh cracks across the broken trail, but the route remained clear. Head upwards where possible.

Curiosity propelled me forward—not determination to reach the summit, but a simple desire to see how much further I might go today. The trail in part felt familiar now, my body remembering a few twists and turns as I climbed steadily upward. And where the night's weather had cut the trail, making it disappear entirely, I carefully traced along the cliff edge, repeating this process until a faded direction was revealed. Each rediscovered section of path felt like a small victory.

I rounded a sharp bend and spotted a figure ahead on the broken track. The worn canvas backpack and faded green jacket were immediately recognizable.

"Jonas!" I called, my voice echoing against the rock face.

He turned, waiting as I closed the distance between us. His face broke into that unsettlingly familiar smile.

"Didn't think I'd see you again today," I said, catching my breath.

"Couldn't stay away," he replied, adjusting his pack straps. "Something about this mountain pulls you back, doesn't it?"

I nodded, glancing up at the peak still hidden in the wisps of clouds. "I was curious if I could get further than yesterday."

"Same," Jonas said. "Ready to push your limits?"

We fell into step together, finding a rhythm that worked for both of us. The trail grew steeper, demanding more from already tired muscles. But there was a strange comfort in the effort, a satisfaction in feeling my body respond to the challenge.

"You disappeared yesterday," I said after we'd silently climbed in silence. "I turned around at the car park and you were gone."

Jonas didn't break stride. "You were busy looking at photos," he said. "Must not have heard me say goodbye."

I frowned, trying to remember. Had he said goodbye? The memory was hazy, overshadowed by the emotions that had overwhelmed me by the end of our hike.

"How do you stay in such good shape at your age?" Jonas asked, changing the subject. His tone held genuine curiosity rather than judgment.

The question struck deeper than he could know, reopening a door to the darkest period after the separation.

"When everything fell apart," I began, picking my words carefully, "I knew I'd need every bit of strength I could muster. Physical and mental."

Jonas nodded, encouraging me to continue.

"A counsellor told me early on—mind and body are one system. You can't heal one without addressing the other." I paused, remembering those first desperate months. "My mind was already susceptible to anxiety and depression. DNA from my mother and an unstable upbringing I lay to blame. If my body was going to survive the emotional pain coming my way, I had to make some hard changes. Also, the counsellor told me this, and seeing my father wilt after separation then dying suddenly a few years later wore on my subconscious. I couldn't follow that path."

"Like what?" Jonas asked.

"First, he said that I had to face alcoholism." The word still tasted bitter on my tongue; an admission of weakness I'd spent years avoiding. "Drinking has become my escape hatch—my way of numbing the pain without actually dealing with it."

Looking back, I realize alcohol was never just a beverage for me, but a shield against feeling. It wasn't dramatic enough to warrant intervention—I functioned at eighty-five percent, sometimes ninety-five, maintaining a successful business and family life for many years. But that missing percentage, that space between functioning and flourishing, harboured the truths I couldn't face.

The real revelation came when my life collapsed around me. Without the protective barriers of marriage, home, and daily routines with my children, I faced a stark choice: confront what alcohol had been helping me avoid, or drown in it completely.

Standing on that mountain trail now, miles from the fridge that once held my nightly escape, I recognize something that took me years to understand: healing demands sobriety—not just from substances, but from denial. Every step upward requires sharp vision, steady hands, and the courage to feel what needs feeling.

As the topic of alcohol was discussed, it became clear that I was now walking away from my old self—the shadow of who I had become. My ex-wife had seen this long ago, along with my signs of anxiety and depression, often intertwined with evening alcohol. She also enjoyed a drink but without appearing to suppress emotions. Exuberance were her celebratory choices with alcohol where mine was consistent and deliberately numbing.

I wasn't a chronic alcoholic, the kind one might picture on the street in tattered clothes, unshaven, begging and with bloodshot eyes. I was a successful business owner, a devoted father who made plenty of time for his family. But it was an issue I chose to keep quiet—apart from the visible empty wine bottles.

I had been unable to deal with my past on my own, and instead, I had brought it into my marriage. Also, realising my ex-wife brought her own issues of which were avoided topics of conversation during our disagreements. The light was always pointed on my business stress and depression at times to blame for the rockiness between us. Never, an acknowledgement of contributory participation to our disagreements with what I saw as a dogmatic necessity for singular control over the family and its direction.

Today, I maintain an uneasy truce with alcohol. I still drink occasionally, but the relationship has fundamentally changed. Each glass represents a conscious choice rather than an unconscious escape. The measure of control lies not in abstinence but in awareness—knowing exactly why I reach for the bottle and refusing to do so when the answer involves running from myself.

This awareness came at extraordinary cost. I had to nearly lose everything—my children, my sense of purpose, very nearly my life—before recognizing that coasting at ninety-five percent still meant missing vital pieces of myself. The tragedy of unaddressed trauma isn't just personal; it ripples outward, touching everyone we love. My children moved away from the father I became, just as I was moving away from the man I had been.

Jonas kept his eyes on the trail ahead, giving me space to continue without the weight of his gaze.

The memory hit me then—not gradually, but all at once. The night when the darkness had threatened to swallow me whole.

———————————— •●• ————————————

The bottle was on the kitchen counter, amber liquid faintly luminous in the dying light. My third for the night—or was it the fourth? The days had begun to run together, particularly after my dream of moving the family to New Zealand was crushed. Drinking to suppress unresolved trauma had always been a component of my life, but it got more serious as time went on, beginning when things with Dianne first began to deteriorate. What had begun as a solitary glass of wine with dinner eventually expanded to two, then a bottle before bed to assist sleep. The boundaries became blurred with the years, and though I wasn't quite so bad as to be considered a traditional alcoholic, I was aware that something was not right. I was living a good business and home life, but that remaining percentage—whatever it was— contained secrets I did not want to know or feel.

I had used alcohol at sixteen to numb the pain of my parents' separation so it morphed into my adult life at times of stress. It worked during its influence, also forcing the suppression of early childhood anxiety living in my body not yet ready to be resolved.

The first few years after my marriage ended, alcohol was not even just about dulling the pain. It was a way of escaping the person into whom I had turned. I'd lost my lucrative business in the divorce, and my kids lived with another person. Gradually, my feelings had dropped to a level where I wore my brokenness on my sleeve. I never learned the art of concealing my feelings. Maybe I was honest, but it was painful for my children. I don't know if my addiction made them feel exposed—not in body, but in spirit. Nothing in what I did was ever intended to hurt them, but the effect was bigger than intention. And during those dark days, the bottle was my faithful companion. I would wake up with a numbed mind, vowing never to drink again, and then the next night open another bottle.

When Michaela came into my life five months after my marriage ended, alcohol accompanied both of us to celebrate our new connection, but I also allowed the numbing for excruciating pain. I tried to hide this reason from her. She never judged me for drinking as we shared it together. I felt an acceptance of the need for regular alcohol. I was a functional alcoholic, although I would not have agreed with that at the time.

It was a vicious cycle—drink to forget, hate myself for drinking, drink to forget that I hated myself. After a few years with Michaela, something began to change, almost imperceptibly. Our celebration for finding each other had slowed and a consciousness around alcohol and the counsellor's advice took hold. Slowly, my drinking eased. A bottle a night dropped to three glasses, then two, and on some nights the bottle was untouched. This controlled addiction lasted for some years but when Michaela left, the cravings returned. I almost went back to the shop for the bottle, my hand automatically reaching out for it in the old routine. And then, for the first time, I understood. If I went down that path once more, I might lose myself forever. I couldn't risk losing everything. I walked out with nothing. It wasn't willpower—it was clarity. I'd been numbing my emotions with alcohol all my life, and if I were going to make it through this, I had to face it head-on.

I needed to feel it all. That night, returning home from the bottle shop whilst feeling devastated Michaela had left, I remained sober, conscious of my own hurt, my own terror, my own possibility. It was the first time in my adult life I chose to face deep suffering without succumbing to the addiction. Withdrawal followed later—an agitation vibrated with a slight longing thirst that couldn't be quenched with an anxiety surrounding all the concerns of trying to start a new life in a shattered mess of failures. But under the pain was pride. For the first time, I was conscious of the silent strength of a man who had persisted in his own pain rather than fled from it. I still drink, but now it is a choice, rather than a habit. Every glass is an option, a deliberate act. The real test is not whether I don't drink but awareness—knowing exactly why I open the top. The toughest lesson was to understand cruising at ninety-five percent meant that I was still missing pieces of myself. Recovery isn't so much from the alcohol; it's from denial. And every forward step requires brave eyes, steady hands, and the heart to experience what must be felt and a preparedness to sink temporarily further in emotional pain with no substance to soften each aching thought.

— • • —

"I had to learn that pain isn't something to be avoided," I said. "It's essential information. Your body and mind telling you something needs attention."

The trail curved sharply right, bringing us to a viewpoint overlooking the valley below. We paused, taking in the panorama of lakes and mountains stretching to the horizon. The beauty was almost overwhelming in its perfection.

"It wasn't easy," I continued. "Changing habits never is. But I started small—clean eating, regular exercise, cutting back on the drinking until I could control it instead of letting it control me. That's when I remembered windsurfing," I told

Jonas as he led the way, his weathered backpack casting a shadow that seemed to stretch beyond the physical realm. We navigated around a huge rock from the previous night's slide, carefully picking our way through the new terrain. "I'd been passionate about it as a teenager. Something about that connection between body, board, and wind spoke to me then."

———————————— •●• ————————————

At the age of sixteen, when the wind and water brought me comfort, I would ride with my gear in tow to Beaumaris Yacht Squadron Jetty, hoping for a strong south westerly to whip up large breaking swells. I'd rig up and swim, dragging my board with the attached rig toward the wind line just past the sheltered end of the hundred-foot wooden jetty.

Water starting in thirty-knot gusts would launch me into the stormy waters, where I'd skim across the surface, sailing one kilometre out in the bay. Mentone Beach a kilometre to shore, where the swells crashed onto the sandbar. I always sought the biggest swells, scanning upwind as they built into white, wind-formed peaks at the centre of my world. If I could survive out there, I could survive the emotional wreckage of family life back onshore.

When Mum was removed, it was just Dad, my sister Julie, and me. An enticing boyfriend soon coerced Julie away, leaving Dad and me with our black kelpie, Sabre.

We lived at opposite ends of the house, meeting only in the kitchen to serve dinner meals. Dad cooked most nights when he wasn't out with a new lady. Perhaps my distance from him stemmed from his role in removing my mother from my life. Was it the same for Luke? Did he think I called the end of his family? If only he had known years ago the origin of that text message of separation—and my desperate attempts to keep his family together.

---•●●•---

The path narrowed, forcing us to walk single file for several meters. When it widened again, Jonas fell back in step beside me.

"It had been twenty years since I'd been on a board," I continued. "I contemplated windsurfing in my early 30s, but a surgeon told me when I was thirty-three that I'd never windsurf again because of my chronic back pain, and I needed a spinal fusion of L4 and L5. Something in the doctor's tone of immediacy for surgery caused me concern, neglecting more therapeutic options such as physiotherapy and massage. But there was something about hitting rock bottom years later that made me think—what if he was wrong?"

Jonas glanced sideways at me. "So, you just decided to try again?"

"Sort of." I smiled at the memory. "First time back, I could barely rig the sail and muscles I hadn't used in decades were screaming. But once I got planning over the water— the rush was a great reunited feeling I was craving, the strong wind in my arms, flying the board over the wind-driven chop and cutting the board around in a jibe—" I breathed deeply, reliving that first rush of spray in my face. "It was like meeting an old friend again. Not easy, but familiar somehow with easy conversation soon following."

"You'd found your element again," Jonas observed.

"More than that. I'd found a purpose—one that my young self-deserved to pursue again. Every windy day meant a new wind to chase, a new challenge to face. The wind and water didn't care about my broken marriage or my lost business or my failures and rejections as a father. It only asked if I was willing to show up today, try again, push a little harder, and go faster than before."

"And you were?"

"Every windy day," I admitted. "Some days I'd sit in the car, staring at the whitecaps, physically sore to move but I'd rig up every time the wind called. Time after time."

"Did it help?" Jonas asked.

I laughed, surprising myself with the genuine sound. "More than I expected. There's something about pushing your physical limits that helps you understand your mental ones better. When you discover you can climb a mountain you thought was impossible, other impossible things start to seem within reach."

•●•

That night, I thought of my younger self, and it marked the beginning—not of healing, not yet, but of the decision to seek it, to fight for it, one strong gust at a time.

The next morning, I looked at myself in the bathroom mirror, really looking for the first time in months. The man staring back was a stranger: hollow-eyed, unshaven, defeated. Not the father my children deserved or who had been complimented in Father's Day cards of the past. Not the man I'd promised that young boy I would become.

I drove to the windsurfing shop, wallet in hand, ready to invest in myself with boards, sails and equipment set for my re-entry into my past life as a teenage windsurfer. I remembered the freedom I'd felt as a teenager, racing across the water and jumping suspended between sea and sky. The pure joy of it, before life complicated everything. I remember as a teen, after Mum and Dad split up, windsurfing at Mentone beach, safe in my world—the wind and water. No conflict, no worry, no loss of security, just my world. I'd yell out in the waves on the third sandbar 'This is the best thing that's ever happened to me!' Something within me was telling me history could repeat.

The wind was brutal, and the water slightly choppy—perfect conditions for what I needed: speed. My muscles protested as I rigged the downhaul of the sail, unfamiliar with the strain required to rig the sail tight for speed. Like getting up from a fall on a bike, my muscle memory took over once I hit the water.

The first run was terrible—unbalanced and uncoordinated, a struggle against both the elements and my own body's weaknesses. But with each attempt, something awakened in me. The focus required left no room for dwelling on losses. There was only this moment, this balance, this partnership with wind and water.

I stayed out until my arms shook with fatigue, until salt had dried on my skin in white patterns like frost. I was exhausted but clearer somehow. The darkness hadn't lifted, but for a few hours, it had receded enough for me to remember there was light somewhere. The water and wind were still my world.

Day by day, I returned to the water. Each session built not just physical strength but a kind of mental resilience I'd lost somewhere along the way. The discipline of it—the need to adapt constantly to changing conditions—became a template for facing life's uncertainties.

On Christmas Day, six years after getting back into windsurfing and just two weeks after Michaela walked out, with no family to celebrate with, I decided to push myself further than ever before. It was a spontaneous decision made at 8.30am and I was on the water at 9.20am. The wind came in early allowing an opportunity for distance. Perfect to remain out on the water. A place that felt more like home. I sailed 424 kilometres in 9.75 hours, averaging forty-three kilometres per hour with only a 10-minute break. It ranked as the top 15th longest distance windsurfed in a day worldwide at the time.

"Why would I come in?" I asked myself as I pushed through exhaustion. "There's no one there anymore. Stay out in your world. It worked as a teenager. Need a hydration drink? Ok, just one, then keep sailing. The feeling of dehydration was more appealing than stepping on land empty of my kids and Michaela."

The physical strain was clarifying despite my emotional weakness after Michaela left. The mind is powerful when in charge of the body. Muscles screaming, hands blistered, skin raw from salt and sun. But for the first time in months, I felt alive. Not happy, not whole, but alive. Windsurfing gave me the opportunity to deal with extreme emotional pain through physical exertion.

The bottle still called sometimes, especially on long nights when memories pressed close. But its voice grew fainter as my body grew stronger, as I learned new ways to process the pain instead of drowning it.

—————————•●•—————————

"It saved my life," I told Jonas, coming back to the present moment. "Literally. There were times when the only reason I got out of bed was knowing I had to get back on the water. When the only thing keeping me from ending it all was the promise, I'd made to be stronger tomorrow than I was today." My promise to my young self in the photo I found in my personal items at my home office years before.

Jonas nodded, understanding in his eyes. "Physical strain can be clarified."

"It gives you something concrete to focus on," I agreed. "When everything else feels out of control, you can still control how you move through the world. How you treat your body. Small choices that add up to something bigger."

We continued climbing, each step demanding more from tired muscles. The path grew steeper, narrowing in places to less than a foot wide etched into the mountainside and, in some parts, non-existent, only leaving us with a general direction to head—upwards, holding onto sharp granite shards and bracing against jagged boulders all conscious movements for a mistake would be the last. But my body responded with a strength that surprised me, finding reserves I just like it had windsurfing that Christmas day.

"Around six years ago and soon after getting back into windsurfing," I said between careful breaths, "I decided to take it more seriously. Started training specifically for GPS speed events."

"How'd it go?" Jonas asked.

"Terrible at first," I laughed, squeezing a sharp handhold. "But I kept pushing. Kept chasing the strongest winds I could find. There's something about that moment when you're perfectly balanced between forces of wind and water trying to blow you down or wipe you out—it teaches you something about life."

We reached a small plateau large enough to relax from the exposure of heights, the trail leveling briefly before the next steep section. Below us, the lake shimmered in morning sun, a perfect mirror reflecting mountains and sky. The beauty of it caught in my eye.

"And now?" Jonas prompted.

"Just days ago, I placed fourth in one of these GPS events," I said, still surprised by my own achievement. "Fourth fastest in the world for my discipline at the time." I have also won a GPS challenge competition competed by windsurfers from mainly Australia and Europe in 2021 and again in 2023. So much for listening to the spinal surgeon! I used my own judgement knowing my body and getting fit.

"That's impressive," Jonas said, with genuine admiration in his voice.

"It wasn't about the ranking, though," I added quickly. "It was about proving something to myself." Curiously discovering of what I was capable. Doing young Mark justice. I had questions on my ability, and I wanted answers.

"That you could still achieve something meaningful?"

"Yes, and that I could transform pain into power and have purpose. Not be broken forever." I gazed up at the next section of trail, steeper and more challenging than what we'd already covered. "That the same forces trying to break me could be harnessed to make me stronger."

We shouldered our packs and started climbing again, the conversation fading as the trail demanded full concentration. My legs burned with the effort, lungs straining in the cold mountain air. But there was joy in the burning, a fierce satisfaction in knowing my body could still respond to challenges, still carry me forward according to my minds will.

"My father died at fifty-seven," I said as we navigated a particularly steep rocky section, grabbing onto the long sharp granite rock for support. "Heart attack, totally unexpected. I was only twenty-two."

Jonas waited for me to continue, seeming to sense there was more.

"Then my mother passed when I was thirty-seven," I added, my voice steadier than I expected. "Motor Neuron Disease. I watched Mum deteriorate, her body betraying her while her mind stayed sharp until the end. My aunty then three years later phoned me one night before Christmas, chatting happily, asking questions about Luke, Olivia, and Dianne before thanking me for staying in touch over the years. I offered to come over to see her for Christmas, which she appreciated. The next morning, I received a call informing me of her suicide. Clearly, she wasn't going to endure the degeneration of the same disease that inflicted itself on my mum after her recent diagnosis."

We reached another small ledge and paused. The valley spread below us like a living map, clouds casting shifting shadows across the landscape.

"That's rough," Jonas said, offering me his water bottle.

I took a sip before continuing. "Having my dad die suddenly, then seeing my mum then aunty then my two uncles all die young of the same disease, it did something to me. Made me realize how fragile all this is." I gestured to our surroundings, but we both knew I meant more than just the scenery. "I promised

78

my young self I'd live differently, that I'd be there for my kids longer than my dad was for me."

"Yet after the separation—"

"I broke that promise," I admitted. "Let myself deteriorate in ways they never would have chosen. The irony wasn't lost on me, even at my lowest."

A falcon circles overhead, riding thermal currents with effortless grace. I watched its freedom for a moment before continuing.

"The day I decided to reclaim my physical health wasn't just about survival. It was about honouring my parents, aunty, and uncles too. Creating experiences my younger self deserved but never had." I adjusted my pack straps, feeling the weight shift. "When I sailed those 424 kilometres on Christmas Day alone, part of me was that little boy who just wanted his dad to take him windsurfing one more time."

"So, the physical challenge—"

"Became the bridge back to myself," I finished. "Each time I pushed past what I thought was possible—embrace one more gust, sailed faster than ever, improved another personal best—I was keeping a promise to that six-year-old kid in the photograph. Showing him that despite everything, we were still here. Still fighting and still sailing."

"It wasn't just alcohol," I told Jonas as we climbed. The trail grew steeper, demanding more concentration. "After the financial separation, I had a substantial sum sitting in an investment account. Started day trading to recoup what I'd lost in the divorce."

"That doesn't sound like dependency," Jonas observed, testing a loose rock before committing his weight.

"It wasn't all about the money," I explained. "It was a rush. The same dopamine hit gambling addicts seek. I'd be driving on the freeway with my laptop open on the passenger seat, making trades worth hundreds of thousands while navigating traffic."

Jonas whistled softly. "That's..."

"Insane? Reckless? Trust me, I know." I shook my head at the memory. "But in those moments, I felt something. Control, maybe. Or the illusion of it. When everything else in my life was falling apart, I could still hope to make money with the click of a button."

We reached a particularly challenging section of trail. Another recent rockslide had altered the landscape, forcing us to pick our way carefully across unstable terrain.

"The thing about dependencies," I continued once we were on solid ground again, "is they all promise the same thing—relief. Escape. A way to avoid facing what's really hurting you."

"But they don't deliver," Jonas said. Not a question.

"Worse than that. They create a whole new set of problems while the original wounds fester underneath." I paused to take a drink of water. "The day I almost lost everything was a wake-up call."

I sat in my rental car, laptop balanced precariously on the passenger seat as I drove down the freeway. My old van was with the mechanic, which was going to cost a lot to repair. I was feeling desperate. The screen flickered with stock charts and trading platforms—hundreds of thousands of dollars in play with each click. My entire wealth, after the divorce settlement, was being wagered desperately to recoup what I'd lost.

This wasn't investing. It was gambling, pure and simple.

The adrenaline rush as the numbers ticked up provided temporary relief from the crushing reality of my diminished life: I had no home of my own, my children shuttled between houses, and the business I'd built from nothing was now sold to strangers. The massive costs of separation proceedings left a small fraction of what had previously been so hard-earned.

The first attempt at financial separation took place in my lawyer's top-floor meeting room, overlooking the affluent heart of Perth. An ex–Family Court Judge had been appointed to oversee the negotiations. Across the table sat Dianne's lawyer and accountant, facing off with mine, all of them discussing the wealth I had generated through my business. The room buzzed with raised voices, assertive hand gestures, and inflated egos—each of them knowing they were about to claim their share of what I had built.

As the arguments dragged on, I found myself scanning the room in silence, calculating their collective hourly rate. Five thousand dollars an hour. I smirked, not with amusement, but with bitter disbelief. I had been blamed for being too stressed at times in marriage, yet here they were—all of them profiting from it. No thanks for the wealth I had created, the same one now fuelling all those engaged morning's income.

That moment of quiet disgust became a turning point. I disengaged my lawyer and carried the three archive boxes of files to the lift as I took back control and negotiated the settlement myself four months later. Serving notice to Dianne's legal team personally in their plush offices was one of the few moments of satisfaction in an otherwise soul-depleting process. A small win, but a win, nonetheless.

I'd check market movements while driving, risking not just financial ruin but physical danger. This behaviour was completely at odds with the careful, strategic businessman and diligent father I'd once prided myself on being. But this wasn't about money anymore—it was about feeling something besides loss.

Trading worked alongside alcohol as my escape hatch, offering the illusion of control when everything else had spiralled beyond my grasp. Each winning trade convinced me I could somehow trade my way back to stability, back to the life I'd lost.

The truth was more painful: no amount of market gains could restore what had truly mattered: my family, my identity as a father who was present every day, not just alternate weeks, and the dream of a stable home for Luke and Olivia.

One particularly narrow escape finally broke through my fog of gambling addiction. I'd positioned nearly everything I had on a high-risk trade, index finger shaking as it hovered over the enter button on my laptop. In that moment, clarity struck with unexpected force: if I lost this, I'd be compromising my future and my children's. The very people I claimed to be fighting for would suffer most from this recklessness.

I closed the laptop without completing the trade. The next day I liquidated my trading accounts and moved the funds to conservative investments. The rush of gambling was replaced by the steadier, quieter satisfaction of knowing I'd chosen responsibility over risk.

It wasn't an immediate transformation. The urge to chase that high remained. But I'd taken a crucial first step toward removing a dependency that threatened everything I still valued.

Pouring alcohol down the drain as a sign of control was mirrored by the liquidation of all trading accounts removing the temptation during weakness.

---·•·---

"Addictions thrive in isolation," I told Jonas as we climbed higher. "That was the pattern I finally recognized. When I felt most alone, most disconnected from purpose and relationship with my kids, the dependencies had their strongest hold."

"So, what changed?" Jonas picked his way across a particularly rocky stretch.

"I had to address the isolation first. Find purpose beyond myself. Create a structure that doesn't leave room for self-destruction." I paused, gathering my thoughts. "It wasn't just about willpower. It was about building a life that fulfilled the same needs in healthier ways."

"Like windsurfing," Jonas suggested.

"Exactly. The physical challenge, the community, the natural high of pushing limits—all of that became a replacement for the artificial escape I'd been chasing." I smiled with a residual feeling of repentance. "I still drink occasionally. But now it's a choice, not a need. The kitchen sink often enjoys the last glass, providing me the satisfaction of being in control. Not something I turn to when the pain gets too intense. The difference now is I don't drink to escape. Before, it was automatic—bad day, take a drink. Stress, take another. Good day, celebrate with a drink. I used to find excuses for every situation to welcome alcohol. I don't touch it when I'm in that susceptible mindset. If I ever feel that pull—the urge to drink because I don't want to deal with something—that's when I know to walk away. Because the second it becomes a crutch, it's no longer a choice. And that's a line I never let myself cross again."

"What about the gambling?" Jonas asked.

"That was hard to kick. It wasn't just the rush—it was the fantasy that I could win back everything I'd lost. Whenever I thought I was close to winning big, I was just sinking deeper. I kept telling myself the next trade, the next bet, would turn it all around. Instead, I was stuck in place, burning through money, time, and trust. I lost months—years—chasing what I'd already thrown away. And the worst part? I convinced myself it was progress with a few winning trades when all I was doing was running in circles."

I shook my head. "Had to accept that some losses are permanent. No jackpot was going to restore my family to what it was. And it wasn't just about losing money.

I was gambling with my future—literally. Like speeding down the highway to go windsurfing, one hand on the wheel, the other refreshing stock prices, convinced I could make a split-second trade that would fix everything. Hundreds of thousands of dollars on the line, my future hanging in the balance with each market fluctuation. It was reckless but addiction convinces you that risk is just part of the game. That moment should have been a wake-up call. Instead, I pushed enter—the draw of false hope greater than the security of less. The trade was open for only a minute before the fear of loss caused me to click Sell. That fifty-minute trip cost around seven thousand dollars. This loss made with this type of destructive behaviour was a blessing leading me to question and finally resolve my gambling addiction."

We reached a narrow granite step and paused to catch our breath. Below us, the valley stretched in emerald splendour, dotted with crystalline lakes. Above, the summit remained obscured by gathering clouds.

"You know what I realized?" I continued, gazing out at the view. "Dependencies are just shortcuts to temporary relief. They promise a quick fix for pain that requires the slower process of healing."

Jonas nodded. "Like taking a helicopter to the summit instead of climbing."

"Exactly. You might reach the same spot, but you miss the transformation that happens along the way. Back then, I wanted shortcuts. Whether it was a quick win in the market or drowning stress in a bottle, I wanted results without the work. Probably because my previous hard work in business was not awarded to me the way I had intended prior to separation. So, I was jaded. Why work again when work didn't pay off for me?

But you can't cheat your way to real progress. You must put in the effort, push through discomfort, and climb—step by step. Addiction halted that for me. It made standing still feel like motion, like I was still in control when I was actually slipping backward."

We resumed our climb, the trail growing more precarious as the rocks beneath our feet felt ready to slip with one wrong weighted step as we pushed past yesterday's stopping point. My legs burned with the effort, but there was satisfaction in the clean paint of exertion.

"The hardest part," I said between careful breaths, "was learning to sit with discomfort. To feel the full weight of loss without reaching for something to numb it."

"Like walking through a storm instead of hiding from it," Jonas suggested.

"Yes. And discovering that you're stronger than you thought and using the motivation of my young self to give him the good life he deserved." I paused at a particularly challenging section, finding secure handholds before proceeding. "The dependencies had convinced me I was weak and needed them to function. But with each one I removed; I found more resilience underneath."

We climbed in silence for a while, conserving energy for the increasingly difficult terrain. The air grew colder as we gained elevation, each breath more deliberate.

"You know what I tell myself now when the urge hits?" I said finally. "When I'm tempted to fall back into old patterns?"

Jonas raised an eyebrow, waiting.

"I ask myself what example I want to set for Luke and Olivia. Even when they're not watching—especially when they're not watching. The man I am when no one sees is the man I'm truly becoming. I also have my morning mirror test."

"A mirror test" replied Jonas.

"Yes, it's deciding on whether you can face the judgement of who looks back at you in the mirror. "

"And what do you see now?" Jonas said, looking at me, giving me a feeling of depth I couldn't place.

"I see a few Marks. Sometimes I can stare back confident that I'm progressing, seeing strength and a renewed health. And sometimes I see a determined man but see through a wanting stare of a better happier life. And if I look long enough, I can see the shattered components of a once proud man. I guess that last look is what I saw needing to return to New Zealand to resolve the remaining broken pieces."

We reached another viewpoint and stopped to take in the expanded panorama. The valley had receded further, details blurring with distance. Yet the perspective gained made the landscape more comprehensible, patterns emerging that weren't visible from below.

"Removing dependencies isn't just about stopping destructive behaviours," I continued. "It's about replacing them with something better. Something that feeds your soul instead of draining it."

"Like what?"

"For me, it started with physical challenges like windsurfing. Also, creative projects—the mental health app I developed. Then reconnecting with people who supported genuine growth." I took a long drink from my water bottle. "The opposite of addiction isn't sobriety. It's a connection to a sustainable form of health."

Jonas nodded thoughtfully. "So, mountain climbing—it's part of that process?"

"In a way. It's a tangible reminder that I can do hard things and besides, I've a fear of heights! That pain has purpose when it leads to growth. And that some views are worth the climb." And besides. I just love this place!"

The clouds shifted momentarily, revealing the summit still far above us. But today, it seemed less intimidating, more inviting—not a challenge to be conquered but a teacher to be respected.

"Ready?" Jonas asked, adjusting his pack.

I nodded, feeling a lightness that had nothing to do with elevation. "One step at a time. And that's why I don't take those kinds of risks anymore. Not with my money, not with my time, not with the wrong people and definitely not with my life. I won't be the guy checking stock trades at one hundred kms an hour ever again. Some mistakes you survive. But if you don't change, one day, you won't."

We resumed our ascent, leaving behind more than just the lower elevations. With each step, the thought of old dependencies loosened further, replaced by the quiet confidence that comes from choosing the harder, healthier path.

Not because it was easy, but because it was worth it.

The ascent dramatically steepened as we continued to climb significantly higher than the day before, pushing past my previous limit until the steep rocky section curved sharply around an outcropping of rock. The new vantage point revealed the summit still distant above us, wreathed in wisps of cloud. Close enough to tantalize, far enough to remain a challenge.

My body froze to the rock, heart feeling a beat of at least two hundred as I stared over the rock edge centimetres from my shaking boot. I could climb to a point, then, with a rush of adrenaline, I'd start focusing on my breath to control my shaking body. I knew my limit and I'd just found it—much higher than the day before but in the same manner. Pushing to the very limit of my capability, feeling one slight move further was a fall into the rock-edged mountainside below.

"This is where I stop today," I said, my breath coming in ragged gulps. "I've found my limit."

Jonas nodded, studying the peak with a thoughtful expression. "You got much further than yesterday. That's something."

"I'm scared of heights. Crazy I'm here, right?" I said to Jonas, my voice full of the recollection. "This exposed feeling at height reminds me of when I was fifteen-years-old, rock climbing on Mount Arapiles in Victoria. It was my first time climbing. I was attempting the climb called 'The Bard' and was close to the top.

I was on a vertical rock wall, just shy of finishing the 5th Belay, as tall as a 35-story building."

Jonas leaned in his eyes intent. "What happened?"

I took a deep breath, recalling the fear. "The rope stuck on a rock below me. I was top-roping, and I couldn't go higher, and I had no idea, ability, or contemplation of how to get down. The other climber at the top yelled down to me, 'Unhook and climb the rest! You're almost there, just a few meters to go!' But there was no way I could. So, I just remained stuck, my legs and forearms pumping, weakening. I felt as if I was losing my grip and falling."

Jonas's stepped closer. "What did you do?"

"I had to ungrip with my hands. I'd let go one at a time each for thirty seconds to shake out the lactic acid that was accumulating in my forearms," I said. "Then I'd change my feet positions to keep them from freezing up. I did this for ten minutes or so while another climber set up an abseil to free the rope underneath me. It seemed to take forever, but finally I could feel the rope loosen so I could ascend to the top. And when I got there, I cried, in absolute relief."

He nodded, feeling the tension. "But you climbed again the next day, didn't you?"

I chuckled, a little shaken by the memory. "Yeah, but this time it was a harder climb. Maybe only twenty stories high, equivalent." I said smiling. "I knew my limits, though just like on this climb. I locked onto the granite, slowing down my breathing, waiting for it to level out. But I knew for certain that was it for me for the day."

We paused for a few minutes looking out over the vast panorama below us. The silence between us was comfortable, and we were each lost in our own thoughts.

"You know what's strange?" I said finally. I feel content stopping here. That's not like me. I'm usually driven to reach the goal, no matter what. But today..." I shook my head, trying to articulate the unfamiliar feeling. "There's a comfort in knowing my limits, in respecting them."

"Maybe that's the real summit," Jonas suggested. "Not some arbitrary point on a map or the top of a peak, but the place where you're at peace with exactly where you are."

I considered his words, feeling their truth resonate.

"We should head back," Jonas said, glancing at the darkening sky to the west. "Storm's coming in."

We slowly began our descent, the trail demanding as much concentration going down as it had coming up. My knees protested each step, but I welcomed the honest pain of physical exertion. So different from the nebulous agony of emotional loss that had consumed me for years.

Back at the car park, I turned to thank Jonas for his company, only to find myself alone. The parking lot was empty except for my rental car, gleaming in the late afternoon sun. Jonas had vanished again, as suddenly as he'd appeared. I figured he'd simply done the same as yesterday. It made sense as again, I was mesmerised looking at the day's stunning photos on my phone.

I scanned the surrounding boulders, half-expecting to see his faded green jacket disappearing around a bend. But only the wind whistled around granite boulders and shattered granite rocks surrounding the car park.

———————•●•———————

The rental car hugged the winding mountain road as I headed back to the hotel. Shadows lengthened across the valley as dusk approached, turning the lake into a sheet of hammered gold. My hands gripped the steering wheel loosely, a subtle tremor in my forearms the only evidence of the day's exertion.

My limit was reached for the second time, and the descent was again without making the peak, but a peculiar contentment settled in my chest. This sensation puzzled me. Just days prior, I'd pushed myself to claim the fourth fastest time ever recorded in a windsurfing GPS speed discipline, driven by the curiosity to conquer my previous Australian record, to prove my self-worth and satisfy my curiosity of ability. Now, faced with another day of an unconquered summit, I felt strangely at peace. The weather report had already made it clear conditions wouldn't allow another attempt during my remaining few days. Perhaps that explained my acceptance.

Streetlights flickered on as I entered the main roads. As I continued driving, I thought of Jonas, and how he had vanished completely. No sign of his faded green jacket among the rocks, no footprints leading away.

I missed his company already. There was something about him—the attentive way he listened, how he seemed to understand and empathise with the journey I'd travelled these past ten years. A journey away from my children, whom I loved desperately but who had grown distant from the once-present father I'd been.

Back at the hotel, I showered, washing away the sweat and grime, then stretched out on the bed, muscles aching pleasantly again. My phone rang. I didn't get many calls as my few friends normally text me. Wondering who it was, I rolled over to my phone on the side table. It was Olivia! My dear daughter whom I had hardly had contact with in the past six months, except a pre-Christmas call to say hi and tell me she was going away for Christmas with her mum and Wayne. She sounded so delightful and happy. Listening, I took deep breaths allowing the love I was feeling to enter to my core. The conversation was quick but contained everything I needed to feel a connection with the daughter I had once been so close to during my family life and time of shared custody.

"Love you, Dad." I heard this making my heart warm and left me feeling emotions of fatherhood that had slowly escaped me with her absence.

That night on the 5th January 2025, sleep came easily until at precisely 3:47 am the next morning. I jolted awake, body vibrating with goosebumps, as tears beginning to stream freely down my face. The realization crashed over me deep in slumber with physical force: my journey had ended. The peace I'd been searching for had found me here in this mountain town, where a piece of my heart had remained for fifteen years.

My phone had lit, waking me up—a text from Luke late in the night Perth time, preceded by Olivia's earlier phone call. Both of my children reached out on the same day I'd climbed that mountain, telling me they loved me. Luke expressed his love in a text with a love heart, just like the granite one on the mountain I had seen with Jonas, while Olivia expressed hers in her soft, beautiful voice. The broken pieces of my soul had somehow reassembled themselves when I wasn't looking but had done so after searching for answers on the mountain the past few days.

I no longer needed to flee Australia feeling unwanted as a father or the life I'd built there. The permission I'd been seeking—to be a father again, in whatever capacity possible—had been granted by the only people who could give it: my dear children, Luke and Olivia. Happy and positive thoughts flooded me about how I could bring Luke and Olivia here someday on holiday, show them the mountains and lakes I'd fallen in love with before the separation text message had shattered our family. I had survived alcoholism, depression, financial ruin, solitude, the loss of my business and a purposeless life.

During the flight to New Zealand, I came across an audio book with the simple phrase "don't give up on your dreams." I thought it referred to business aspirations, as business back home was tough, but now I understood: my deepest dream had always been to be a father. The persistent text messages of love I'd sent Luke and Olivia over the years, even when met with silence, had finally reached their hearts. My mind then wandered to Elli as I lay in reflection.

"I believe in you," Elli had texted after I sent her a photo from my highest point on the mountain. I had found my limit, but also my reason. Elli knew just glimmers of my journey and reason for my travels back to New Zealand to hike, searching for answers and direction. She helped provide me strength to pursue my dream of peace and acceptance.

Fate would bring me to Elli. Or, as it was commonly phrased, the universe had brought us together. The first time I saw Elli, I walked past her, my eyes captured by her warmth and beauty. Our eyes met, and an immediate connection radiated through my heart. She was a gorgeous, slender brunette with straight, just-past-shoulder-length hair that flowed, highlighting her smile. I felt a need—something deeper than lust—to introduce myself to Elli. From that moment, it wasn't a romantic relationship that commenced but a spiritual connection that remained in the physical encounters, one deeply relevant during my recovery from Michaela's departure.

I used to meet Elli for coffee every couple of weeks, which sometimes stretched to every couple of months, but whenever we saw each other, compliments flowed effortlessly, and there was a genuine warmth and care between us. My bond with Elli deepened during my trip to New Zealand. She sent messages of encouragement, knowing I was searching to find peace.

It was January 2nd, 2025. I was at the airport, preparing to depart on my search for meaning. I messaged Elli and asked her to send me a warm photo of herself—something to look at when I needed positive energy. Throughout my hikes, I often thought of Elli, drawing strength from her words and believing in myself. Each day, I found myself surrounded by butterflies and crickets not only natural to the mountain hiking environment but in the spiritual world —good luck charms I came to call "Ellihoppers" and "Elliflies." Elli was a butterfly herself. I would chuckle, imagining her saying, "Good luck to any man trying to catch this butterfly." She was a free spirit, belonging to no one, conforming to nothing. I loved that about her. She spoke her mind, and it was always something beautiful and interesting.

My hikes involved sending Elli photos and sharing my thoughts, no matter how emotional they were. She gave me strength, responding with encouragement and advice—reminding me to remove my boots and feel the earth's energy directly. Elli was deeply spiritual and a non-conformist—refreshing, open to deep conversations, emotions, and connections. Elli and I shared a close connection despite barely knowing each other. I knew of her heart more than her life story. I respected her immensely for her generous empathy and unconditional warmth during tough times.

Whenever I had walked with Elli, I'd find my arm around her, compelled to feel her energy as we had conversations about life, its meaning, our experiences, and our beliefs.

Elli was also a rebel, a free spirit that wouldn't be held captive to the typical thinking of most ladies of her age. One time we walked to get pizza and approached the intersection with a button to push for safe crossing. "I'm not pushing that," Elli would say with all her energy. "If I want to cross I will. I'll do it on my terms. I simply won't be told what to do." Elli then smiled with a cheeky giggle and skipped across the road like a young girl knowingly rebelling for the first time.

For all her beauty and pure heart, Elli had a deep vulnerability from her past that would appear randomly in gesture and word. It was obvious Elli had past traumas of her own that had once damaged her heart. She would only hint on her past, preferring to focus on her growth and spirituality or mine. I never inquired too deeply on Elli's vulnerabilities as butterflies are delicate and need only the slightest of fear to never return.

I believe Elli's history formed her into a butterfly never fully trusting anymore. And would never stay in one situation too long for fear of being trapped and moulded into something for someone else's game. It was a privilege to be invited to be trusted by Elli. into her world and able to share such a meaningful connection especially in such a poignant time of my life.

Elli left my life as quickly as she came into it touching me so briefly then disappearing like butterfly's do into the world—her world. I imagine Elli continuing her journey flying a spiritual path touching other souls with her beauty and pure heart. I love Elli's heart and told her this. Perhaps that was enough and touched a fear of connection causing her to take flight. Elli had an authenticity, innocence, and uncontaminated beauty. To me she was the second angel that I've ever met in my life. The first being Michaela. I will forever be grateful for her brief care when I needed it most.

---·•·---

Perhaps the greatest summit isn't always the one visible from the trailhead. Sometimes it's the journey itself that matters most.

7

FIND YOUR TRIBE

The importance of community in surviving the darkest moments

I woke with strange clarity, my mind made up about the day ahead. The weather forecast called for deteriorating conditions—a large front moving in that would bring heavy rain and winds by mid-afternoon, far more severe than the previous day's spasmodic gusts and brief rain squalls. The sensible choice was to explore the lower-elevation trails, something gentler on my already taxed muscles.

I packed my daypack with this easier hike in mind. Again, ensuring bananas, peanuts, protein bars, three water bottles, and my passport were in the back pocket. My body appreciated the prospect of a recovery day after two consecutive pushes toward the summit. Logic dictated I save another summit attempt for better conditions.

Yet as I drove toward the trailhead for the forest walk, an odd restlessness gnawed at me.

The small coffee caravan on the main street beckoned as it had previous mornings, but perhaps caffeine would settle my indecision this time. I joined the queue, breathing in the rich aroma that cut through the crisp morning air. The barista worked methodically, her hands creating art with practiced precision.

"Double shot cappuccino, please," I said when my turn came.

"Sugar?" Her accent was distinctly Kiwi.

"Yes. Thanks."

Coffee in hand, I stepped aside to make room for the next customer. The line was growing since I'd arrived, pushing me toward the edge of the footpath.

"Double shot cap", she called. A warm smile was passed down from the van along with my coffee. As I lifted the cup to my lips, I happened to glance up.

Through a break in the buildings, the mountain revealed herself. Her jagged peak pierced through a collar of clouds, stark against the blueing sky before the impending change coming later in the day. Something about the sight stopped me mid-sip. The mountain that had dominated my thoughts for days looked different somehow—not more accessible, but more inviting.

I stared, feeling an inexplicable pull. It was not necessarily ambition to reach her summit, but a sense that she wasn't finished with me yet. That there were things she still wanted to show me, conversations we needed to finish.

A shiver ran down my spine, similar to the tremor I'd felt during my middle-of-the-night epiphany. The mountain wasn't just rock, ice and ancient geology. She was a voice I needed to hear, a teacher I wasn't done learning from.

The forest hike suddenly felt like avoidance. The mountain was calling me back, not to conquer her, but to listen more deeply.

I drove straight to the now-familiar trailhead, sipping the coffee that was alerting my body for another gruelling but epic climb. The parking lot was empty—other hikers heeding the weather warnings forecast to be worse than the periodic storms the previous few days. I laced my boots with purpose, checking my pack one final time, again always making sure my passport was in the top pocket for identification in case of the worst.

"Back again?"

I turned to find Jonas leaning against the first trail marker, dressed in the same faded hiking clothes as yesterday. He looked as if he'd been waiting, though I hadn't seen another vehicle arrive as I prepared my pack and laced my boots.

"Couldn't stay away," I admitted. "Thought I'd try for the forest trail, but..." I gestured toward the peak, now partially obscured by clouds again.

"She's got a grip on you," Jonas observed, adjusting the straps of his worn pack.

"Something like that. Guess you're heading up too?"

He nodded. "Curious to see how far is possible today."

We fell into step together, retracing the now-familiar trail start. The first kilometre passed in comfortable silence, our breathing finding a synchronized rhythm.

"What brings you back?" Jonas finally asked as we navigated a rocky section. "Not many people try three days in a row, especially with the weather moving in and the forecast worse than the last few days."

I considered the question, searching for honesty. "Hard to explain. I feel like I'm supposed to be here. Like there's something more to learn."

"From the mountain?" Jonas replied.

"From myself, maybe." I paused at a small, smooth boulder, taking a drink from my water bottle. "Yesterday you asked me about keeping my body strong. This morning driving up to the trailhead I've been thinking about what kept me weak."

Jonas waited; his gaze steady but not demanding.

"After the separation," I continued, "I felt a solitude that reminded me of when my parents separated. It was uncommon back then and I felt like a leper with friends unable to start a conversation about my change in situation. Sometimes with energy, then to have nothing to say."

"Because you lost half of your time with your kids?"

"Losing them was the main reason. However, the separation was also from the social aspect of parenting. The BBQs, kids' parties, dinners out with parents and afternoons spent at the beach or park with other families from the kids' schools. Then there was the loss of who I thought was my best friend. My ex-wife."

A separated father is not a popular person I discovered with whom I thought were friends. Other dads who we had entertained and even gone on holidays with never bothered inquiring on how life was going. I could tell they were emasculated to the point of not pursuing a relationship with a single man in fear their wives would disapprove. These were the wives who headed into the night with my ex-wife after separation. These were never friends I realised, just drinking acquaintances met due to the kids' schools and their social activities.

The school drop offs were difficult with parents walking past knowing your personal tragedy without the courage to say 'hi' or make eye contact. Some of these people were previously welcomed in my house, dining to feasts and wine on my financial efforts and swimming with their kids in our pool. I was outcast socially and personally. I was alone, mateless in a place I wanted to leave and now half of my life without my dear kids. This state of mind weakened me as I had no support, except the bi-weekly counsellor visit. The loneliness pulls you in, unable to operate with normal confidence. It's quite disempowering, especially after feeling a sense of success with business and being needed by my kids all the time.

Jonas slowly shook his head in disbelief.

As Jonas and I continued our climb up the rugged mountain trail, my thoughts drifted to how windsurfing had become my lifeline after the separation. The physical challenge, the rush of harnessing the wind's power gave me a sense of control when everything else felt like it was spiralling.

We paused, leaning on a large granite boulder to catch our breath, and Jonas turned to me with those perceptive eyes that always seemed to see right to the heart of things. "Windsurfing became more than just a hobby for you, didn't it?" he asked, taking a swig from his water bottle.

I nodded, a wistful smile tugging at my lips. "It saved me, in more ways than one. Not just because of the endorphin rush or the distraction, but because of the people it brought into my life. People who shared the passion for wind and water and some of whom could understand in some way what I was going through. Some guys were reliving their youth like I was, and a few were also dealing with difficulties resulting from their life traumas. Sharing our issues that gave a bond in addition to sharing the buzz of an adrenalin filled windsurfing session."

Jonas then settled onto a small accommodating rock, his posture open and attentive. "Finding your tribe," he said simply.

"Exactly." I gazed out over the sprawling valley, memories washing over me. "I remember this one morning, about six months after I started sailing again..."

---·•◦•·---

The beach was deserted as I pulled into the parking lot, the early morning sun reflecting blindingly off the wind-swept water. White caps everywhere ready to host my session. I rolled out my sail I would shortly be using—the bright blue, orange, and red sail I would be using in mere minutes, its colours bold against the muted beachfront. This sail that would shortly be as familiar to me as my own face, a reminder of my rediscovery after so many years away from the sport that had dominated my youth. The wind whipped across the sand, stinging my cheeks and sending bits of sea foam skittering. It was the kind of morning that made most people burrow deeper under their covers: a big cold front backed with strong powerful wind.

But for me, it was perfect.

Undressing in the cold was a familiar feeling from my young teenage years at Mentone Beach in similar winter conditions. After school, I would ride home to collect my already-packed windsurfer on it's purpose built timber trolley and speed to the beach not wanting to miss the strong winds in fading afternoon light. I shrugged deeper into my wetsuit, a feeling that gave me comfort knowing I was about to get wet and sail. The cold bit at my exposed feet, but I barely felt it. All my focus was on the wind blowing up small white caps anticipating the speed to be had and the cry of gulls wheeling overhead.

As I started hauling the rest of my board and gear from my VW Golf, a flash of movement caught my eye. There, at the far end of the car park also surrounded by tall Norfolk pines, was another figure. Fit-looking, rigging his own sail, his movements efficient and practiced.

Curiosity propelled me forward. I didn't expect to encounter another soul out here, especially on a morning like this. But I was relieved, as I had never sailed here before. As I drew closer, the man glanced up, his gaze immediately drawn to the GPS watch on my wrist.

"Giday," he called out, a grin splitting his wind-chapped face. "You sailing in the GPS speed comp too?"

Surprise rippled through me, followed quickly by a rush of camaraderie. "Speed for sure but I don't know of any comp" I confirmed, closing the distance between us. "I was hoping I wouldn't be the only one out here today."

He laughed; the sound was snatched away by the wind. "Cody," he said, extending a hand. His grip was firm, his skin weathered in the way of someone who spent more time on the water than land. "Just getting back into it?"

Something clicked into place then, a sense of rightness I hadn't felt in longer than I could remember. "Mark," I said, matching his grin. "Good to meet you Cody, and absolutely!"

Cody stood in front of me in his wetsuit, harness on and a real smile breaking across his weathered face. He'd one day become more than a sailing friend but a lifeline—my first call on my darkest day, his steady presence and rock-solid loyalty the cornerstone of my new tribe.

We rigged our sails side by side, in the bone-deep chill and the unforgiving wind. Conversation flowed easily, the way it does between kindred spirits. By the time we hit the water, I felt lighter than I had in years.

The splashes of cold felt like an electric shock as I walked out a few meters to launch into the wind-swept water, but it barely registered past the initial shock. All my focus was on the sail snapping taut, the board racing forward as I caught the first gust hooking into the harness poised firmly in the foot straps. Beside me, Cody let out a whoop of pure joy, his form a study in power and grace—something I would aspire to attain after my 20-year layoff.

We sailed until the wind allowed. Pushed each other to go faster, sometimes checking our speeds in comparison. It was a race without personal competition to catch the most elusive gusts and get the fastest speed each of us could. And in those few windswept hours, something shifted. A sliver of hope took root, fragile but stubborn.

If I could find moments of transcendence out here, in the harshest of conditions, maybe I could find my way through the rest of the wreckage too.

———————————•●•———————————

"Cody became more than just a sailing buddy," I told Jonas, coming back to the present. "He was proof that survival was possible. That there was life on the other side of the pain."

Jonas nodded, understanding softening his features. "He showed you that you weren't alone."

"More than that," I said, emotion thickening my voice. "Through his sailing ability and kind actions towards me, he made me believe I could be strong again. He invited me into his tribe. The team he was on was in a windsurfing team. Part of a world windsurfing competition that saw 1000's of competitors compete around the year in various windsurfing disciplines all based on speed. And that the same winds that were my teenage saviour could also now be the key to rebuilding."

I turned to face Jonas fully, needing him to understand. "Finding your tribe, your people...it's not just about having others to lean on. It's about seeing your own resilience reflected back at you. Being reminded of your capacity to endure. To transform."

Jonas held my gaze, something like pride flickering in those enigmatic eyes. "And that made all the difference?"

I thought of the years since that fateful morning. The competitions I won, the laughter shared, the records broken, the overnight stays in Albany and the friends made. The slow, painstaking work of piecing myself back together.

"All the difference," I confirmed, my throat tight. "I would not have made it this far without that reminder. Without Cody, and the others like him who showed me there was a way forward for my life."

———————— • ● • ————————

It was 5:15 am the morning after Michaela had left when I awoke to a silence so dense I could hardly stand it. My stomach was churning in sickness of the reality that I awoke to. Faint sunlight filtered through the window in Olivia's old room where I chose to sleep the night Michaela walked out, casting itself over the single bed I found myself in. Her absence from the home had immediately turned the home into a building. Just walls, floor, and a roof. It was an emptiness I could feel.

I reached for my phone and pushed, with my shaking finger, Cody's number mechanically.

"Cody," my voice barely whispers, "I'm not good."

He comprehended immediately. I can't recall anything he said, if anything at all.

I dropped my phone, got up and drifted through the house in a trance the only comprehension of finality. If this was actually my last day on earth, I wanted a final coffee. There was no milk in the refrigerator, so I drove to the 24-hour market, selected a carton with mechanical detachment, paid without glancing into the eyes of the cashier.

I drove back detached from reality, ghost-like except for knowing my dear Michaela whom I'd spent eight wonderful years with had left forever. The feeling tightened my stomach increasing my sickly feeling. Turning into my driveway I could see there was a police vehicle parked next to the verge.

I stopped and lowered my window knowing why they were here. "You're here for me," I said, a fact, not a question. "Are you Mark?" a smartly dressed female police officer's gentle voice inquired as she walked up to my van. "Yes." I replied. Her colleague followed her a few steps behind calmly saying "Mark, we're with the police. Cody called triple zero, and we're here to make sure you're safe. He told us what's happening with you and is concerned for your life. Will you come along with us to the respite hospital, please? We just want to make sure you get some help and stay safe."

I felt an immediate relief, as if I was reconnecting with basic humanity. The kind words from the two policewomen, their warm and concerned gestures, and my mate Cody's quick thinking broke my trance. I snapped out of my semi-conscious state, ready to make my final cup of coffee and then end things, knowing it would finally relieve the overwhelming agony that had built up over the years. I was *completely ready to surrender my life, to just go inside, have that last coffee, and end it all.*

But then I broke down coming into consciousness, slumping over the steering wheel crying uncontrollably. The relief of human comfort and care collided with the crushing reality that I had lost my dear Michaela forever whilst my kids had drifted away.

The street was deserted, especially at this early hour. I felt relieved that I could break down in some privacy, in my van, on an empty street, just outside my house. I agreed to go to the respite hospital but would do it independently on my own terms. I had made it in life this far, and it felt empowering to drive myself, even with the patrol car following in the street lights behind.

The journey was taxing. I'd look in the rearview mirror reminded of the severity of my health and the reasons it had disintegrated. I missed my kids and Michaela, felt completely hollow and had no reason to continue, but somehow found myself driving. It was only five kilometres, but it felt like I was driving to my own execution, knowing drugs would be prescribed. I feared that they would turn me into a shell of myself. If I wasn't that already, I knew I'd be worse. My plan seemed better, at least I'd be in control. I almost turned around, but then I visualized the photo of my younger self, the one I'd promised a better life to.

With that, I arrived at the hospital parking lot, feeling completely broken. I couldn't function, couldn't think anymore. Cody had been right. I needed immediate help. I broke down again, unable to console the overwhelming devastation that had taken over me. It was as if every form of separation had merged into a singular, unbearable pain. My family, my kids, my business, my dreams, and now Michaela—all gone. The only thought left was, what had I done wrong? Did I really deserve all this? They were the only logical thoughts remaining as I walked toward the hospital doors, now ready to receive any treatment that would save my life.

A woman came outside the hospital doors into my blurred vision, and I hoped she was there to greet me and help. I couldn't make out the few words spoken to the two policewomen who had helped me walk, now holding me up in front of the lady. My swollen and wet eyes couldn't make her out clearly, and my ears were deaf to anything except my own painful thoughts of failure and loneliness. The only thing I could soon feel was the policewomen beginning to guide me away from the hospital doors.

Then, I heard the soft voice of the young police officer who had first asked if I was Mark. Her caring tone alerted me to what she was saying.

"We have to take you to a different hospital, Mark, before you can come here. Once you're assessed, it's possible to come here, but it won't be until Monday."

I had heard and felt enough. Understanding that being offered to be taken to General Hospital by the two policewomen brought back memories of previous years of drugs that left me numb with no rehabilitation to deal with past childhood and adolescent traumas. Ones like separation from my mother as an adolescent, then difficulties with my mother's relationship and my father dying young leaving no leadership for how to live a life. I would rather die than go back to that drugged life. Just like since the day I received a text message of separation I would never have another drug to manage my mind ever again. I will do it on my own without pharmaceutical intervention. Mental illness is common. It's no longer hidden the way it was many years ago when my mother would've appreciated a diagnosis and appropriate medication. The reason I chose not to have pharmaceutical intervention one moment passed my text message to separation, was that it ignited something in me, I already was deep down aware of. I needed to grow as a person, or at least try, as opposed to just rely on the numbing effects of a pharmaceutical drug. I think they have merit to allow the mind to settle when cognitive learning and recovery can occur after deep trauma are appropriate. But simply to remain stagnant and drugged wasn't for me.

With these thoughts spinning, I'd reached my capacity for agony and collapsed meters from the door on the footpath. The concrete sidewalk initially felt cold and unyielding beneath me as I collapsed outside the respite hospital. Too exhausted, too broken to take another step. My body pressed against the rough surface, its grainy texture scraping my cheek. The symmetrical brick pavers stretched away from where I lay, their reddish pattern blurring in my vision. Beyond the concrete curb, yellow lines on the asphalt road wavered and distorted, their bright warnings seemingly mocking my situation. I was vaguely aware of the small patch of struggling grass nearby, a pathetic reminder of life continuing despite my complete shutdown. The two officers stood over me, their shadows shifting as the hours passed, while the institutional buildings loomed in the background. I remained frozen on that hard ground, unable to move forward yet refusing to enter a system I feared would destroy what little remained of myself.

"I'll die here first," I thought, my body refusing to budge from the sidewalk.

I lay motionless for close on two hours, as the respite hospital doors remained closed, with the two officers standing guard over me. The morning sun rose higher, crept slowly across the parking lot, providing a faint warmth to the concrete beneath me. In the odd limbo between despair and resignation, I again recalled the vow that I had made to my younger self as I drove to the hospital—the child in the photo who was worthy of more than this. This recollection provided the strength I needed to first lift my head, stand to walk, and then to drive myself home where Cody had asked other members of our windsurfing crew to meet for my support. They remained with me through those initial critical phases, a human shield between me and the darkness.

"Without them, I wouldn't be here," I said to Jonas, my voice firm despite the heaviness of the memory. "They saved my life in the most literal sense."

We sat in silence for a long moment, the weight of understanding hanging between us.

Later, I would remember the aftermath of that desperate night when Michaela left—how I collapsed outside the hospital the next morning, unable to be admitted. I had refused the public system, unwilling to be medicated again. Years earlier, I'd experienced a severe reaction to medication prescribed for anxiety. I had what was called a "fit" one night and was taken to the hospital. From that point, I was placed on a path of monthly psychiatry appointments and pharmaceutical sedation that numbed rather than healed me. I wasn't going back to that version of myself. Numbness didn't work. I wanted to be real—dead or alive—but not dulled into submission.

That morning outside the hospital, I was seeking respite. I collapsed not from weakness, but from complete exhaustion—of spirit, of hope, of meaning. I believed, then and now, that my depression and anxiety were born from unresolved childhood traumas, then triggered by separation from my family life and especially kids, not from some fundamental unrepairable flaw in my chemistry.

The breakdown worsened in the days that followed. I remember vividly the first afternoon I returned home after working at my business to an empty house. No Michaela. No family noise. Just silence echoing through rooms that used to hold life.

Grief swept in with brutal efficiency—first for Michaela, then for everything unresolved that had been buried beneath layers of survival. I hadn't truly processed my parents' separation when I was young, or my father's choice to end his marriage by distancing me from my mother. And now, I was experiencing something eerily parallel—an unravelling of my own family life and distance growing between me and my kids.

For the first time, I saw it all clearly: the grief for my mother, the weight of my father's decisions, and my own fears about repeating painful patterns. My father had his reasons—his health was declining, and he did what he thought was necessary. But his decision left me unanchored in a critical stage of life. When he remarried and moved away, I was left alone in the family home at eighteen. He passed six years later, and I now realise that I never fully grieved that loss either.

At twenty-two, I was lost—no guidance, no real mentorship, only mistakes piling up in business, in love, in life. Michaela's departure, though shaped by its own complexities and my contributions to them, reopened every abandonment wound I had ever carried. It was another trusted presence, gone. The result, regardless of circumstance, was the same: a crushing loneliness.

I walked through the front door that afternoon and collapsed just inside it. My knees buckled, and I dropped to the floor, as I had a few days earlier outside the respite hospital. That moment marked one of the lowest points—when I felt stripped of everything: Michaela, my children, my strength. My bond with my kids, once my greatest purpose, had faded over time, and my role as a father had become uncertain. It was a moment not just of heartbreak, but of complete disorientation.

Jack, my neighbour, found me there. We'd lived next to each other for four years and had discovered we shared the same school history, twenty years apart. Over time, he became a close friend—almost a surrogate father figure. Michaela and I had often shared meals and laughter with him.

Jack saw something in me that I couldn't see in myself at that moment. He valued my life. Over the following week, he checked in daily. He brought food, made sure I ate, and kept me company. His sister, equally kind, came over to help. Together, they ensured my home stayed safe from temptation and that I wasn't alone.

That night, after Jack left, I sat in the dim light of the lounge, staring at the Christmas tree. Photos of Luke and Olivia still hung from the branches. But the ones of Michaela and her boys were gone. And so was the one of us together.

I sat there unable to comprehend it all—how I had come to lose everything I loved most. My children, my partner. I wasn't perfect. But I knew, deep down, I was a good man. That truth, no matter how buried, would become the foundation I'd have to rebuild from.

———————•◦•———————

It was a week after Michaela moved out that she left a message for me.

"Hi Mark, I want to collect my belongings on Saturday. Is 9-12 noon ok with you?"

"Of course," I replied, mentioning I would not be there leaving her the privacy of her friends to help without the distraction of my presence.

That Saturday morning, I drove by an adjacent street where I could see Michaela's and other cars in the driveway of my house, taking furniture and belongings. I watched for a few minutes after hoping she wouldn't show up. Texting me instead of her change of mind. Wishful thinking, and now no kids and no Michaela. Driving back to the house with not a sign of her was one of the hardest days I've ever experienced. If it weren't for young Mark and my decision to give him the best life he deserved, these words would not have been written.

A growing thought cemented in my mind the following year after Michaela left. Michaela's choice to leave without returning indicated our relationship had run its course. Couples can recover from trauma, but only with mutual desire. Michaela's decision not to reconnect or rebuild despite our love and deep history echoed what my heart had been telling me—the situation was killing it. It didn't want the life with Michaela back in the same way Michaela didn't want to return.

My heart had known this truth for some time, refusing to let me continue down a path that would have led to an even more uncomfortable future—one surrounded by children who weren't mine and, eventually, grandchildren who weren't either. If I were going to have kids in my life, they would be my own or none.

My DNA couldn't reconcile the conflict.

Maybe that was a flaw in my character. Or maybe it was a testament to my devotion and purpose as a biological father. I chose to believe the latter. I hadn't chosen my DNA, but I had spent the later part of my life walking a road that opposed it—almost to my breaking point.

My heart had spoken.

So had Michaela's.

------------•●•------------

When Jonas finally spoke, his voice was gentle but resolute. "Seems to me that's the real lesson here," Jonas said finally. "We can't control the storms that hit us...but we can choose our fellow sailors. The ones who won't let us capsize, no matter how rough the seas get."

I nodded, too choked up to speak. He was right, of course. Finding my tribe, my port in the wildest storm...it hadn't erased the pain or magically fixed what was broken.

But it had given me an anchor. A lifeline to cling to when the waves threatened to drag me under.

And as Jonas and I shouldered our packs once more, ready to tackle the next stretch of our climb...I realized that's exactly what he had become too.

A reminder that even in the deepest valleys, on the steepest slopes...we're never quite as alone as we think we are.

Not when we learn to recognize the kindred spirits in our midst. The ones who see our scars and choose to walk beside us anyway.

8

KEEP SHOWING UP

Patience, worthiness, and the quiet power of consistency

As Jonas and I climbed higher, the air grew colder, each breath biting. The trail narrowed to a rocky ledge, a sheer drop-off on one side leaving no room for error. We moved carefully, our focus telescoped to the next handhold, the next solid place to plant a foot.

There was a metaphor in there somewhere, I thought gently smiling to myself. Something about the necessity of measured steps, of deliberate forward motion when the path ahead seemed impossibly difficult.

We reached a small outcropping and paused to rest, gulping down lungsful of crisp mountain air. Jonas leaned against a sun-drenched rock; his gaze pensive as he studied the patchwork of green far below.

"You know," he said after a pause, "for all the talk of chasing dreams and pushing limits, sometimes I think the hardest part is just showing up. Day after day, even when it feels like you're getting nowhere."

I followed his gaze, my own thoughts turning inward. "Patience," I murmured, more to myself than to him.

Jonas cocked his head, curiosity sparking in those knowing eyes. "How so?"

I broke off, breathless, then continued. "At the time of the split, I was negotiating to take over another business." There was still a sting to the memory. "Getting text messages from the seller while I was on the phone with my legal advisor negotiating the separation process. 'Hey Mark, one half of the business sold, but the other is still for sale.' Could have picked it up for stock value by the end."

Jonas paused, allowing me to go on.

"But with the separation underway, there was no direction to go in. My legal advisor counselled against making any significant financial manoeuvres mid-proceedings. All business options—just vanished." I shook my head at the bitter irony. "That business would have fit perfectly onto my current one. The synergy would have been amazing, and the family would benefit. Would have done everything differently. Done it anyway. I was always going to lose in the end, so fulfilling my capabilities would have been an enjoyable process to see unfold."

I kicked a loose stone, seeing it roll off the edge. "Rather than growing, rather than building something new, I had to wait. Years waiting for the opportunity to search for business possibilities again. All on hold while the financial separation lingered. It was like I was being starved for the opportunity to move forward. Constant delays in proceedings and agreement for close on two years all whilst my offer of 50/50 was made to allow us both to move separately but evenly."

My voice dropped. "New Zealand was the bigger dream, though. Had it all mapped out before the separation—ten acres, good schools for the kids, outdoor activities. The perfect place to start over. But that dream unravelled too." I felt myself repeating my frustrations spoken earlier to Jonas, but I continued needing to vent.

Jonas glanced at my face. "That must have been tough."

"Worse than difficult. It was as if the way to a better existence had been suddenly cut off. Something I'd been planning for years, something that might have transformed everything—gone." I motioned toward the peak above us. "You can see a destination so clearly, but the path vanishes. And there's nothing you can do but wait, hope that one day you'll find another path there."

I continued to ascend, each step with a purpose. "In the meantime, my top priority occupation became a part-time father. The rest—business, New Zealand, travel, personal goals—everything took second place, sandwiched between custodial weeks. I needed to make them feel they were worth waiting for, so I needed to try and be worth waiting for, too."

Jonas nodded slowly. "So, you put your dreams aside in order to give them priority."

"Exactly. I couldn't just check out or walk away from what was most essential. Had to be present every week, even when not having their custody, be their dad —even if it was going to mean watching other things go by." I searched Jonas's eyes. "And I had to have faith that if I waited long enough, those things would come around again someday. That waiting wouldn't mean losing everything." I paused on a tiny rocky protrusion, holding the weight of a decade in stasis. "The toughest part wasn't so much waiting—it was holding onto the hope that the waiting would be worth it. What could possibly be better than family life close to my kids? That someday I might be able to rebuild not only my relationship with them, but my own life as well."

Understanding softened Jonas's features, but he remained silent, giving me space to continue.

"I tried to stay positive during my weeks with the kids," I pressed on, the words tasting bitter even now. "Plan adventures, make the most of our time. But as they got older, as the silences stretched longer...I started to doubt myself. Wondering if I was doing enough."

The admissions hung heavy in the thin air, truths I'd rarely let myself acknowledge. Saying them aloud felt like cleaning a wound—painful, but necessary for any real healing to begin.

Jonas regarded me steadily, compassion warming his gaze. "That must have been incredibly difficult," he offered, with no trace of judgment in his tone. "Feeling like you were losing ground, even as you fought to maintain connection."

I blew out a shaky breath, surprising myself with the relief his validation brought. "I kept reaching out, even when there was no reply. Texting jokes, sending photos of our past fun times, and leaving voicemails saying I love you. Anything to keep the line open, to let them know I was still here. Still their dad."

A slight smile tugged at my lips. "It got to the point where my phone contacts might as well have read 'Luke—will not respond' and 'Olivia—doesn't want to talk'. But I didn't let myself stop trying." I knew they must be struggling, which agonised the distance between them and me, but I couldn't see them. The circumstances my kids were placed in created an emotional distance between us—something neither they nor I had any real control over.

"Because giving up would have meant accepting the distance," Jonas supplied, perceptive as ever. "Admitting to yourself that you were losing them."

I swallowed hard, my chest aching with the truth of it. "I couldn't bear that. Couldn't let myself believe this new reality was permanent. So, I kept showing up, kept putting myself out there...even when it left me exhausted. Heartsore and simply broken. Some days, it took everything I had just to hit send on those texts, to keep my voice light on those unanswered calls."

I knew Luke and Olivia were hurting from their circumstances, trying to cope with their own disrupted lives. They were focusing on whatever certainty and security they could find, even if it meant accepting distance from their father. They had to be loyal to themselves first—not me, not their mother. It's nature's way of surviving, I thought. Although their silence felt so painful to endure, I understood it was never their fault.

"Did you ever stop?"

"No, continued calling, even when there was silence."

A memory surged forward, sharp, and clear as mountain water.

---·•●•·---

The post office lady stamped the package, pushing it back to me across the counter. Inside, wrapped tightly in tissues, was a framed list of life lessons—36 of them. Words I had spent weeks crafting, honing everything I wanted to say to Luke myself as if I would never be able to say them to him. It was like my last ability to influence my son.

"Want tracking on that?" the clerk asked.

"Yes," I nodded. "Please."

It had been nearly a year since I'd last laid eyes on my son. Many months of unanswered texts and calls that went straight to voicemail. But in a few days was his twenty-first birthday—his induction into official adulthood. My last chance, perhaps, to speak into his life as his father before the world completely claimed him.

I watched the package vanish into the back room of the post shop, praying Luke would even open it. Praying he'd notice the desperate hope embedded in each well-written sentence, each lesson gleaned from heartache and struggle.

"He'll get it Monday," the post office lady told me, handing me the receipt.

"Thank you." I was relieved as that was his birthday.

A few weeks earlier, I had reached out to my ex-wife via email before Luke's 21st birthday, suggesting that our joint gift to him be our presence—standing together in unison as his parents on his coming-of-age day. I wanted to give him even a small sense of healing, a moment of support to help ease the burden of the separation he had endured.

Her response was lengthy. I didn't read it all. It was about her, not Luke.

Luke was my only focus. I had been searching for just one word: "yes." But as I skimmed through the message, all I saw was resistance. An unwillingness to give him the one gift I thought he truly needed and deserved from both of us.

• ● •

Monday evening came around, I was in my own kitchen, stirring pasta. Steam rose in lazy curves, evaporating with basil and garlic. Outside, night began to fall over the neighbourhood, streetlights starting to cast a warm, amber glow over the street.

That day, Luke turned into a man. I wondered whether he was going out with his friends, his mother, Olivia, and Wayne. I wondered whether he felt happy and loved. I wondered whether he recalled birthday mornings of his boyhood—waking him to pancakes fashioned to resemble whatever currently captured his heart: dinosaurs, cars, soccer balls. Would he remember me?

The pot boiled over unexpectedly, hissing as water splashed onto the stovetop. I was just about to turn down the heat when my phone flashed on the benchtop.

My heart skipped a beat as Luke's name flashed on the screen.

I opened the message with trembling fingers, bracing myself for disappointment. But instead:

"Thanks for the gift, Dad. Really appreciate it. The lessons resonated. Hope you're doing well."

My legs gave way. I sat slumped on the kitchen floor; pasta left unchecked. Tears blinded my eyes, stinging and surprised.

He opened my 21st present. He read my messages of love and advice from his father.

In one blazing moment, joy surged through me—pure and overwhelming. I replied to Luke with all the love I could fit into a message, flooded with relief just to be in contact with my dear son on his 21st birthday. But like a dam breached, that joy gave way, and behind it came the flood of sorrow that had been waiting to spill.

Because in all the years of fighting to save Luke, of shouting down silence, of trying to be the father he required—I had lost Michaela.

Beautiful, gentle Michaela, who had hugged me through the darkest nights. Who had loved me through the brokenness. Who I'd tried for years to keep sheltered from the deepening black hole of loss consuming me from the inside out.

Before I could think better of it, I was texting her:

"Luke messaged me tonight. For the first time in nearly a year. Today is his 21st. I'm so sorry I lost you in the process. Miss you every day."

The reply came sooner than expected:

"Great news, Mark. Congratulations to you both. Keep going, no regrets."

Her text was gentle, but unmistakably distant—the voice of someone who had long since stepped through a door and quietly closed it behind her. And in that moment, I finally saw what I'd been unwilling to face: Michaela hadn't just left four months ago for her good reason. The separation had begun long before, unfolding silently through small but growing signs of disconnection. Her decision may have come suddenly, but its roots were deep in the slow retreat of her once-warm affection.

I began to reflect on moments that had troubled me—times when I felt unseen amidst my own grief. She encouraged me to attend milestones for her boys—their birthdays, their celebrations, dinners with their partners—at a time when I was still quietly aching for my own children. I'd suggested she could meet her boys at her place where they lived with friends, hoping she might sense the pain I was *carrying, but my house we had shared had become her space, and I was left to wrestle with conflicting loyalties in silence.*

I felt a particular tension around Luke—my own son. Though distant from me at the time for reasons I couldn't fully understand, his absence didn't lessen the sense of disloyalty I felt within myself for showing up so fully in celebrations that weren't his. My heart told me: if there are to be 18th or 21st birthdays or family dinners, they are for my children. That truth was in my bones. Ignoring it cost me more than I realised.

It reminded me of my younger years—of a moment when my father, newly remarried, seemed to favour his wife's son over me. The issue was trivial, but the message stung. He declined a small request of mine, choosing instead to prioritise someone else's child. At the time, I felt cast aside, and I vowed never to let my own son feel that way. But had I done the very thing I once resented? I hoped not. Luke had always mattered to me, even in his silence.

Michaela's early compassion for my grief over my children had slowly been replaced with a more pragmatic view of our life together. And maybe, in her eyes, that was a natural progression. But for me, the shift was deeply painful—made heavier by my own inability to voice my truth. I stayed quiet, tried to be strong, and in doing so, ignored what my heart desperately needed to say. Years of emotional suppression left me raw.

The tears came then—not just for Luke's unexpected message, which felt like a ray of hope, but also for the truth I could no longer deny: the woman I loved had let go. Whether gently or abruptly, she had stepped away and perhaps found comfort elsewhere. My heart had known this before my mind could admit it. And maybe, in my grief, I had been trying to outrun a reality that was always catching up.

Our love, which had been at the heart of my rebuilt life, was now an edge—a painful complication rather than a joyous future.

The water on the stove had boiled off the pasta, and the bitter smell of charred food finally roused me from the floor. I stumbled up, turned off the burner, and shepherded the ruined pot to the sink, where it hissed in cold water.

Two texts on my phone. Two lifelines. One restored, but tenuously. One severed for good. I saved Luke's message, deleted Michaela's, and ordered a pizza.

Some nights, that's all the victory you can manage.

Jonas remained quiet for a long moment his expression thoughtful. When he finally spoke, his words were careful and measured.

"It sounds to me," he began, "like you were proving something. Not just to your kids, but to yourself."

I frowned, not tracking his meaning. "How do you figure?"

He fixed me with a look that seemed to strip away all pretence. "You were showing yourself that you were worthy of your children's love. That even if they pulled away, even if they didn't respond...you were still their father. Still the man who would move mountains to be there for them."

Emotion clogged my throat, sudden and fierce. I blinked rapidly, turning my face into the wind to hide the sheen in my eyes.

"Most people," Jonas continued gently, "they let the rejections pile up. Let the unreciprocated effort convince them to close off, to protect their tender places. But you...you absorbed the disappointment, the loneliness. Took it on as part of the deal, the price of admission for the privilege of being their dad."

A shaky laugh escaped me, half wonder, and half grief. "I'm not sure that's anything to admire. Might just make me a glutton for punishment and a persistent failure."

But Jonas shook his head, conviction firming his jaw. "It makes you a man who understands the real meaning of unconditional love. The kind that keeps giving, keeps showing up...even when it's not able to be returned in kind. The kind that knows patience isn't just waiting around for something to change—it's choosing, day after day, to be steadfast. To hold the door open, no matter how many times it's slammed in your face."

The lump in my throat grew, threatening to choke me. I swallowed hard, struggling to form words around the riot of emotion in my chest.

"I wanted to give up and disappear into a different life," I confessed hoarsely. "So many times. Wanted to let the exhaustion, the fear of another rejection, win out. So, I could escape thinking that no hope was better than keeping the glimmer of light alive. But every time I thought of throwing in the towel...I pictured this moment. Sitting with them as adults, trying to explain why I let their silence push me away. Why did I stop fighting for every inch of closeness?"

I met Jonas's gaze dead on, letting him see the certainty that had crystallized in my bones.

"And I knew, with everything in me...that's not the story I want to tell. Not the legacy I want to leave. So, I kept texting. Keep calling. Kept showing up, even when it felt like shouting into the void."

Jonas's eyes met mine with a depth of understanding that spoke volumes. "You kept proving your worthiness," he said simply. "Not just as a father...but as a man who knows his own value. Who refuses to let external forces define his commitment, his capacity to love unconditionally."

We sat with that for a long moment, the weight of it settling into my marrow. When Jonas spoke again, his voice was soft but sure.

"The lesson here, I think...is that patience isn't passive. It's a daily renewal of faith—in ourselves, in our loved ones. A willingness to keep our hearts open, even when the world tells us to close up shop."

I nodded slowly, clarity seeping in like sunlight through fog. "It's showing up," I murmured. "Even and especially in the silent stretches. Trusting that our steadiness may be a chosen anchor, a lifeline...whenever they're ready to reach out and take hold."

Jonas smiled, pride and affection warming his gaze. "Sounds like wisdom hard-won," he acknowledged. "The kind that only comes from walking the path, even when you can't see the destination."

"Even when you're not sure there is a destination," I agreed slowly nodding. "Just the knowledge that the journey is worth it. That they're worth every blister, every blind corner."

We lapsed into a comfortable silence then, each lost in our own thoughts. I gazed out across the sheer void beside the narrow trail, fixated on a falcon gliding effortlessly below us. Its wings cut smooth lines through the air, each movement an elegant study in precision and purpose.

It hovered with such grace—but also urgency. Hunting to feed its chicks. To survive.

I thought, *that was me once.* I used to comb through trade magazines, scanning for manufacturers and brands to represent in my wholesale business. It wasn't glamorous, but it was instinct—providing for my family, building something solid beneath our feet.

But after the separation, that role shifted. It felt like my wings had been clipped. Despite remaining loyal to my children and working hard to provide, I no longer returned to the same home. I continued to 'hunt' in the way I always had, but now it felt like I dropped the spoils at the door forced to walk away.

There was an unspoken expectation that the lifestyle we once shared would continue seamlessly, even though everything had changed. I was still absorbing the pressure, still carrying the weight—yet what once defined me was now framed in criticism. The same drive I brought to business, once admired, had become a flaw.

I reached a point where I could no longer bear the emotional cost: to give endlessly yet feel removed from the family I was trying to support. Half the parenting time. Half the memories. Half the presence.

I began to feel that if I was no longer welcome in the same role, perhaps it was time for others to learn how to carry it. To take on the hunt themselves. To be as successful as I had been—not as punishment, but as a necessary part of the life that had been chosen.

I wonder sometimes if the kids noticed how their dad stopped flying. How the invisible cape—Super Dad, the one who could do it all—quietly fell away. I think they did. The silence in those in-between moments said enough. And that's what hurt the most: when the cost of clipped wings was paid not by me, but by the kids.

After a moment, Jonas hauled himself to his feet, brushing dirt from his well-worn pants. "Ready to get back to it?" he asked, hefting his pack with a wry grin. "Trail's not getting any shorter."

I groaned good-naturedly, my own joints protesting as I stood. "You're a regular beacon of encouragement, you know that?"

But even as I grumbled, I felt a new lightness releasing my limbs. A sense of purpose, of renewed commitment to the climb.

The sun was high overhead as Jonas and I approached another ridge, pausing to catch our breath and take in the vista sprawling before us. The valley floor seemed distant now, the lush greens and blues muted by a haze of afternoon light. Up here, the world felt both endless and intimately close—a reminder of how far we'd come, and how much further there was still to go.

Jonas took a deep gulp from his water bottle, his eyes narrowing against the glare. "Gotta say," he mused, "something about being up here puts things in perspective. Makes the worries down there seem a little smaller and more manageable."

I followed his gaze, my thoughts skipping back to the early days after the separation: the raw panic, the crushing uncertainty, and the bone-deep knowledge that my kids needed me to be their rock, even as my own foundations were crumbling.

"Consistency," I said softly, more to myself than to him. "That's what got me through those first few months. The promise I made to my young self—and to them—that no matter how much the world shifted beneath our feet...I would be their constant. Their North Star to navigate by. I will always be a dad."

Jonas cocked his head, curiosity gleaming in his eyes. "Easier said than done, I'd imagine. Especially when you were navigating your own upheaval."

A muttered laugh escaped me, carrying more weight than humour. "Understatement of the century," I acknowledged. "There were days I could barely get out of bed, let alone muster the energy to be the Super Dad. But I knew...I knew that the one thing my kids needed most was stability. Consistency. Some signal in all the noise that they could count on if they chose to."

Memory tugged at me, insistent and vivid. I let it wash over me, the details still sharp-edged after all these years.

———————— • ● • ————————

It was a Thursday afternoon, three weeks after Dianne had moved out and my week with the kids in the family home. I was standing in the kitchen, staring blankly at the handful of takeout menus I'd unearthed from a drawer. Grocery shopping had fallen by the wayside, the fridge a barren wasteland of expired condiments and wilted produce.

Exhaustion dragged at my limbs, a bone-deep weariness that had little to do with physical exertion. The act of choosing a restaurant, placing an order, and making small talk with the delivery person—it all felt monumentally overwhelming, an Everest of mundane tasks.

A small voice cut through the haze, tentative but tinged with excitement. "Is it pizza night, Dad?"

I turned to find Luke hovering in the doorway, his grubby soccer uniform hanging off his thin frame. His hair was messed, his cheeks flushed from practice...but his eyes held a fragile hope, a quiet plea for normalcy amidst the chaos.

In that moment, everything crystallized with painful clarity. This right here—this was the front line. It was the place where I could provide some semblance of solid ground for my kids to stand on.

I pasted on a smile, ignoring the way it felt brittle and false on my face. "Sure is, mate. Thursday tradition, right? What do you think—ham or sausage?"

Luke's face lit up, the shadows receding just a bit. "Both!" he declared, bouncing on the balls of his feet. "And extra ham. And garlic bread!"

And just like that, we fell into the familiar rhythm—the banter, the playful negotiations, the ritualized comfort of our Thursday routine. Never mind that it was just the three of us at the table, Olivia happily feeding the little dog Arnie pieces of ham she'd allocated to cool down. Never mind that I could barely taste the food, each bite sitting like sawdust on my tongue.

What mattered was the light in Luke's eyes as he recounted a goal he'd scored at practice, the easy laughter that bubbled up as we fought over the last slice, and the fleeting but precious sense of normalcy, of continuity in the midst of upheaval.

Consistency, I thought as I watched him chatter animatedly and Olivia feeding her little friend, their troubles momentarily forgotten. The life raft we cling to, even as the storm rages on.

The cruellest lesson of separation wasn't loneliness or even financial devastation—it was discovering that no one cares about your intentions. The world judges outcomes, period—kids included. No matter how pure my motives or how genuine my desire to protect my children and preserve some semblance of their childhood security, results were all that mattered.

When Luke stopped speaking to me, what struck me wasn't the years we'd spent practicing soccer together or the time I'd spent teaching him to ride bikes. What registered was his current pain, his current anger. When Olivia chose her mother's side in conflicts, my history of bedtime stories and patient homework help, painting, or cooking with her counted for nothing against immediate emotional comfort.

I fought something primal—another man inserting himself between me and my genetic legacy with my ex-wife's encouragement. Nature over hundreds of thousands of years has designed fathers to guard their offspring not just from physical threats but from competing influence. How was I to know, let alone trust, his values, behaviors, and attitudes that were to influence my young kids? Every cell in my body recognized Wayne as an invader, yet civilization and my ex-wife demanded I accept this invasion with good grace.

The sense of replacement cuts bone deep. Children need stability, routine, consistent presence—everything divorce destroys. So, they adapt, finding these essential elements wherever available. For Luke and Olivia, increasingly, this meant their mother's home, where daily life continued with minimal disruption, where a new male figure provided what I was allocated at her choice to offer only part-time.

What nobody tells you about shared custody is how quickly you become unnecessary. Not unloved perhaps, but functionally superfluous. The children's world continues turning without you for days, then weeks. They develop inside jokes you don't understand, routines you're not part of, relationships to which you remain forever peripheral or unknown.

I had built my entire identity around being needed—as provider, protector, and guide. Coming face-to-face with my dispensability shook foundations I hadn't known existed. No matter how fiercely I loved them or how carefully I planned activities during "my" weeks, the harsh truth remained: they were managing quite well it seemed without me most of the time.

This realization broke something fundamental in me—not immediately, but gradually, erosion rather than earthquake. Each time Luke declined a call, each time Olivia gained enthusiasm about going back to her mum's house, another piece crumbled away.

What saved me wasn't pretending this didn't hurt. It was accepting that outcomes rarely match intentions, no matter how perfectly executed. That sometimes all your love, all your effort, all your sacrifice buys you nothing but the private knowledge that you tried your absolute best with what you had.

---•●•---

"I realized then," I told Jonas softly, "that stability wasn't about providing a perfect life. It was about being present, being predictable...even in the smallest of ways. I tried to show up, repeatedly, even when I was running on fumes. Being the safe harbor, they could choose to count on, no matter how high the waves climbed."

Jonas nodded slowly, understanding etched into the lines of his face. "Kids have a way of finding their footing," he murmured, "when they know what to expect. When they can trust that certain things will remain constant, even as the world shifts around them."

"Exactly." I blew out a breath, the tightness in my chest easing just a fraction. "It wasn't easy, especially in those early days. There were times I thought I was doing more harm than good, that my efforts to maintain routine were just a flimsy band-aid over a gaping wound."

I shook my head, old doubts and self-recriminations flaring briefly. "But I came to understand that consistency isn't about pretending everything's okay. It's about providing a framework that kids can rely on even in turbulence. It's showing them that even when things are at their darkest...there are still some lights they can count on to guide them home even when they decide not to walk the path."

"It wasn't always enough," I admitted hoarsely. "There were times the gulf felt too wide, the wounds too deep for any amount of pizza nights or weekend rituals to bridge."

Jonas was quiet for a long moment, his gaze distant as he absorbed my words. When he finally spoke, his voice was soft but laden with conviction. "You gave them a foundation," he said simply. "A solid ground to stand on, when everything else was shifting beneath their feet. That's no small thing, Mark. It's the very essence of fatherhood—the steady presence, the unwavering support...even when you're barely keeping your head above water."

Emotion clogged my throat, sudden and fierce. I swallowed hard, blinking against the sting in my eyes.

"I also failed."

"How so?" said Jonas, taken aback.

Well, even as a young boy, Luke had a strong will. His defiance was never simple rebellion—it was a sign of a developing sense of self. I remember one early morning when he was about four years old. It must've been 6 am and Luke was riding his little tricycle inside the house making a little bit too much noise for Olivia still being asleep and his mum most likely, too. I asked him to stop because people are sleeping. He didn't. He kept riding around glancing up at me, ignoring me, fixated on his early morning ride around the stairway and back around the corridor. I raised my voice slightly without making too much volume that may wake Olivia and her mum. I said, "Luke enough."

He continued to ride doing one more lap before proceeding to then ride his little tricycle up to the other side of the island bench where I was making a double shot cappuccino with one sugar. My morning ritual. He got off his bike, stood up so he could just see me over the other side. I peered over the island bench bar and saw his beautiful blonde hair with his cute little face looking up at me, undeterred by my instruction. He looked directly at me and said, "Sometimes I'm just not going to do what you asked me to do." He turned and got back on his tricycle ready for another lap. I was shocked and I didn't know how to respond for a moment as his comment was digested.

"I've got to play this very carefully," I said to myself, hiding my smile, admiring his spirit. I don't want to extinguish that spark. I want to harness that, but that attitude needs guidance and respect. I went up to Luke around the bench and held his dressing gown, preventing him from riding any further.

"Stop," I said, probably just loud enough to wake Olivia and her Mum. Something I was trying to initially prevent Luke doing. Funny. Luke got the point, and I was proud how I handled the situation sipping my coffee soon after.

However—during my custody week a few years into separation, I lost control. Luke and Olivia were staying with me. Luke was still young, around fourteen, and was still absorbed in his Xbox long after I'd called him for dinner. I'd asked him a few times, gently at first, then more firmly, wanting him to eat while dinner was still warm. He didn't respond—until he finally did, with frustration and resistance.

Tired, emotionally raw, and worn thin, I walked over, reached out and placed my hand on the back of his neck—not in anger, but in an impulsive attempt to interrupt the standoff and guide him toward the table. Still, it was the wrong approach. It crossed a line.

Looking back, I believe that moment changed something between us. The quiet trust we'd built—a thread that had held through so much—began to fray. He needed reassurance and gentleness in a time of upheaval, and instead, I reacted with control when what was required was compassion.

I could list the reasons—exhaustion, grief, the emotional landmines of separation—but none of them undo that moment. I lost my footing. And in doing so, I chipped away at the father he had always seen me as. The man he looked up to—the one who seemed invincible—had faltered.

What I didn't fully realise at the time, and only came to understand later, was that I may also have lost a piece of his respect. Not irreparably, I hoped—but enough to explain in part the growing distance that followed.

There was something else that night I couldn't ignore. Alcohol was in my system. It wasn't the cause, but it didn't help. That incident cast a hard light on its place in my life—and I knew something had to change if I wanted to remain the kind of father he deserved.

A sudden thought occurred. My mother's bipolar manifested at times in violent outbursts and a highly emotionally charged presence. My dad sometimes asked me, "What mood's your mother in?" when he came home from work. My reaction would be a shrug but be internalized as, "You're the man. Find out for yourself then tell me whether I should stay home or leave."

I didn't respect my father's position on this. He was the man of the house. Assessing on his behalf the emotional stability of my mum wasn't my job. I understood my mother was difficult and I think that's why he gave up drinking in fear of what he might do to her out of pure frustration. He was never going to leave his home because of her. He chose to have Mum removed instead. Leaving himself with me and my sister.

In hindsight, I sometimes wonder if my ex-wife struggled with how I embodied the role of "man of the house." Maybe it was the way I steered our move to Perth when Luke was just six months old. Or that I launched a business and chose to keep those decisions largely my own. Looking back, I can see how those choices—though well-intentioned—may have left her feeling sidelined.

Perhaps that's why New Zealand never happened. She'd already made a major move for us once, and maybe the idea of uprooting again—especially on my suggestion—felt like too much. Even if I believed it would benefit the kids and our family as a whole, I realise now that the cost to her sense of autonomy may have been too high.

Our eventual separation and divorce seemed to confirm how deeply these tensions ran. I remember the advice a neighbour once gave me—leaning over the fence with a knowing smirk: *"Just say yes, dear, and you'll live a peaceful life."*

Maybe he was right. But I couldn't do that. I couldn't suppress who I was or what I believed in just to avoid conflict. I wanted partnership, not passivity. When it mattered, I stood my ground—not with anger, but with clarity. I made my case and hoped we could meet in reasoned debate. That's exactly what I tried to do on our last evening in New Zealand—searching for a shared vision, one final time.

"My mother could be physical with me at times when I was young. I remember one moment vividly—around age ten—when I asked if my friend Jason could stay for a sleepover. Without warning, she grabbed me around the front of my neck telling me how unreasonable it was to ask that particular day. That moment stayed with me."

Years later, I saw echoes of that moment in myself. Not the same force, not the same place—but till a loss of control. I'd reached out to guide Luke away from his Xbox after multiple reminders to come to dinner. It was meant to be gentle, just a nudge. But I know what he felt. I know what I became in that instant—not the father he trusted, but someone unpredictable.

It wasn't violent, but it broke something between us. I had repeated a pattern I never intended to. My mother had bipolar disorder. I was dealing with grief, emotional fatigue, and leaning too much on alcohol to cope. Different reasons, perhaps—but the same impact.

Luke needed me to be stronger than I was. He showed me that in his withdrawal, in his silence, in the slow drift of absence that followed. I can't fault him for that.

I wasn't always worthy, no matter how pure my intentions. But I always tried. I tried to act with love. I tried to earn back the respect that moment had cost me. And I still do.

"You can't always win, Mark. And your intentions were always trying to," Jonas said gently.

I nodded; my eyes fixed on the ground. "It's just... ironic. The same rejection I once directed at my mother has come full circle—done to me."

"How so?" Jonas replied.

"My household as a child was often at the mercy of my mother's moods." I had moved out and was living independently after my father sold the family home. I had just returned from a whirlwind trip to America—Queens, New York, the Bronx, even a wild detour through Tijuana. I'd been eager to share the stories with Mum. We hadn't been close for some time, but part of me hoped that the distance between us might have softened.

I rang the doorbell. She opened it with a glare, her expression already laced with blame. "You didn't even send a postcard," she said, voice sharp and cold. And then, without pause, she slammed the door in my face.

Something inside me buckled—some hidden girder finally giving way after years of strain. The years came rushing back. The damp sheets clinging to my skin as I lay frozen in the dark, afraid to breathe too loud. My heart pounding in my chest as voices rose through thin walls—cups shattering, plates breaking, and the desperate silence that always followed. I had become fluent in the language of their chaos—decoding the slammed doors, raised voices, and sudden silences into meanings I was too young to fully grasp: their rage, their helplessness, the tension that filled every corner of my mind.

One night, I remember voices again—different this time, louder, more urgent. I was a boy, barefoot on the carpet, drawn out of bed by the chaos unfolding down the hall. Through the narrow slit of my bedroom door, I caught a glimpse— Tony, my dad's friend, carrying Mum out of the house and into a waiting car. Her limbs limp, her head back. Days later, I saw her again in a hospital bed, drugged, vacant. I barely recognised her.

It's no wonder I quit competitive athletics as a young teenager. My nervous system was already spent. The adrenaline I once relied on to compete had been drained long ago—burned out by years of late-night stress responses and emotional landmines. Before the starting gun even fired, my body had nothing left. I had to pull out of the finals of a state championship unable to comprehend another adrenalin moment. That last marked the end—I wasn't just exhausted, I was emptied. I was fourteen. Only much later did I see it clearly—my first brush with anxiety had come from the one person meant to soothe it: my mum.

In a moment I still carry shame for, I lost control. The door—solid, unyielding— bore the brunt of what I'd never said. I kicked it. Once. Then twice. Hard. Then harder. It didn't move, but the act itself made something shift. I stood there trembling, hollowed out, my breath caught somewhere between fury and sorrow. Then I turned and walked away, stunned by the storm still living inside me.

As I drove away, the tears came. Then the phone rang. It was Dianne. "Where are you? What have you done? The police are looking for you."

Later that day, the police called. Mum had reported me. Not long after, she dropped the charges. But a week later, a letter arrived. Carefully written in black pen, it said she was disowning me as her son.

That letter brought me back to another moment—when I was eighteen, and my mother showed up at my rental, asking to move in. She'd rented out her place and needed somewhere to stay. I said 'no', as she stood on the porch holding her two suitcases. No explanation, no room for argument. Just a simple boundary forged out of years of emotional exhaustion. I closed the door. And cried.

In that moment, I had become another person who couldn't live with her. It must have been devastating for her. And perhaps, years later, slamming the door in my face was her way of answering that moment with one of her own.

I believe my mother lived with a condition that caused her extreme, deep inner struggle. She fought silently through life. Never able to live with self-acceptance and abandoned at times by all close to her.

I've rejected, and I've been rejected. The reasons may be different, but the pain is the same: a parent and child, separated.

That thought stayed with me as I placed my next foothold high in the mountain. The air was thin, but it was the past that made me feel unsteady.

Abandonment is not something that merely occurs; it's a physical sensation that burrows its way through your body and festers. When I was standing on the streets of Perth, holding that text message among the crowds, what hit me initially wasn't sadness or even anger—it was shock of acknowledgement. The hollow pit in my stomach, the aching lightness as though the earth had disappeared beneath my feet, the peculiar sense of my skin being too tight for me—I had experienced these feelings with every molecule of my body since childhood. The day my father told me that my mother was to be removed from our house, I felt that same physical disintegration, that same severing loose of what I thought was permanent.

Now, years later, my body remembered before my mind could register what was happening. That awareness brought with it my greatest fear: that Luke and Olivia might also carry trauma in their bodies—just as I had.

The true fear of abandonment isn't in the initial shock. It's in how it rewires your understanding of love. How it teaches you that the things you hold dearest can vanish without warning. It trains you to hold back, to never fully trust, to always listen for the sound of someone walking away.

This was the inheritance I'd spent years trying to stop at my generation—the emotional weight I swore I'd never pass on to my children. And yet, despite everything I gave as a family man and father, there it was: unfolding in real time, delivered in a text message from their mother.

Over time, a new and gnawing fear began to take root—the fear that my silence with Luke was not just circumstantial, but intentional. That his absence held an unspoken message. Without contact, I was left only with distance and my own questions. Was it shaped purely by disappointment in me? Or perhaps— consciously or not—by influences from the household he now primarily lived in?

I didn't know. And the not-knowing hurt most of all. Because what I wanted more than anything was to be someone Luke could still turn to. Not perfectly, not always—but enough.

Luke was approaching the same age I was when my father died suddenly of a heart attack. I couldn't shake the fear that history might repeat—that he might lose his father at an early age, just as I had.

Like Luke and me now, my relationship with my own father had been strained after our family broke apart. But three months before he passed, something shifted. We began spending time together again. Just small pockets—a few hours a week—walking Sabre, the dog we shared between our homes, or going out for dinner.

When he died, the tension between us was gone. There was love. And that brought me a kind of peace that I would carry for the rest of my life.

What haunted me was the thought that if something happened to me— unexpectedly, as it had to my father—Luke might be left holding onto animosity. That would be a catastrophe for him. A cruel, unfinished narrative.

I was desperate for reconnection, not just for my sake—but for his. So that if anything ever happened, Luke could grieve with clarity, not regret. That he'd remember his father as someone who loved him, always. And that the closing chapter between us would be one of closeness, not conflict.

My mind flashed to Olivia—to the quiet desperation in her eyes that last afternoon before I released her fully into her mother's care. The way she clung to me, her thin arms wrapped tightly around my shoulders, as if she could stop the inevitable through sheer force of will.

"In the end," I continued haltingly, "the greatest act of consistency was also the hardest. Realizing that Olivia needed more than I could give her on my own. That the back-and-forth was doing more harm than good, fracturing her sense of stability at a time when she needed it most. It had to become consistency of love... at a distance."

I drew a shuddering breath. The memory was still razor-edged, even after all these years.

"Letting her go, fully and without condition... that was the ultimate test of my commitment to her wellbeing. It meant putting her needs above my own fierce desire to hold on—to keep gasping for every scrap of time and connection."

Jonas laid a hand on my shoulder, the warmth of his palm seeping through my shirt. "I can only imagine how difficult that was," he murmured. "Choosing to step back, to sacrifice your own heart for her sake."

A sad smile tugged at my lips, the ache in my chest deepening. "It went against every instinct I had," I said softly. "Every fibre of my being screamed to fight— to demand my rightful place in her life. But I knew... I knew the kindest, most responsible thing I could do was to give her the gift of certainty. A primary home. A stable foundation on which she could rely."

I paused, the weight of it settling between us.

I shook my head slowly, grief and wonder tangled in my voice. "The great irony is this—sometimes the most loving thing we can do is let go. To accept that our role will change, that our influence may fade... but our love never does. That we can remain a quiet presence in their lives, even from afar—even when it tears us apart to hold that distance."

Jonas still with his warm hand on my shoulder, his expression soft with something like pride. "You were her true north, Mark. Even when you couldn't stand beside her, your steadiness never left. Don't ever doubt that she felt your devotion—felt it in the spaces between the visits, the silence between the calls."

His words sank in like a balm, soothing wounds still raw beneath the surface. I swallowed hard. "I hope so," I murmured. "I hope when she looks back, she sees a father who never gave up—who showed up however he could, even when that meant stepping back and trusting the roots we planted would hold."

Jonas gave a small, knowing smile. "She will. That kind of love doesn't vanish. It weaves itself into who they become. It becomes strength they can reach for—especially when the way forward gets dark."

We fell into a comfortable silence, the valley stretching wide beneath us, long shadows stretching toward the horizon. But inside, something had shifted. A warmth spread through my chest—a quiet assurance anchoring itself where doubt used to sit.

I had tried to be constant. Sometimes I failed. But I had shown up with all the love I could manage. I'd tried to be a North Star in their sky—dependable, steady, always there even when unseen. Maybe, in the haze of everything, they had seen me more like a setting sun—once warm and close, now dimmed by time and distance.

Still, I kept shining. However faint the glow, I kept showing up in the only ways I could, hoping that one day, when they needed it most, they might glance up and remember... I was always there.

9

REBUILD YOURSELF

Choosing growth, purpose, and identity after collapse

The faded mountain trail twisted like a thread of determination between granite sentinels, worn by time and the weight of those who had passed before me. Wind carried the scent of the impending storm—sharp, metallic, promising transformation. Jonas moved ahead, his weathered backpack casting a shadow that seemed to stretch beyond the physical realm.

"Purpose isn't discovered," he said, his voice cutting through the mountain silence. "It's excavated from the bedrock of your deepest pain."

I caught up, my breath ragged. "Sounds like something you'd find on a motivational poster."

A knowing smile flickered across his face. "Truth often sounds simplistic until you've been crushed enough to understand it."

My mind drifted to Indore, a central city in India. To the moment my mental health app—message4support—first took shape amid the chaos of my disintegrating life.

·•·

By April 2014, an apathy to life back in Perth took hold. I wasn't interested in anything apart from the kids. I was sitting in my business, wrestling with a moment of desperation. What if I could push a button on my phone and have Dianne appear, saying, "Hey Mark, just put it back. It's not good for you."

This has reference to a wine at night that was developing into a bottle after we didn't move to New Zealand. And I lost interest in business and, to be honest, in Dianne after she refused to try New Zealand and then started going out at night in Perth to socialize more with her friends. She still expecting me to remain motivated to provide the luxurious life whilst my choice of motivation was the quiet semi-retired type in the mountains of New Zealand. Stress a distant memory replaced by slower secure life in nature. Drinking increased fuelling my apathy and discontentment.

That was my magic moment.

I set about developing my mobile application called message4support. I went in deep, working day and night for months. Goosebumps of inspiration regularly consumed me. I wasn't just going to sell cosmetics anymore. I was going to change the world.

By chance, I met Kuldeep, a director from an Indian IT company whose staff had been emailing my wholesaling business for the past year. He was a young man about 35—clean-shaven, polite, wearing thongs that seemed an interesting combination with a suit for a business trip. But when he spoke about his firm, which employed over four hundred staff back in India, I was impressed.

Two coffees later, we shook hands. Kuldeep was confident they could develop my project at a significant discount to any Australian IT firm. I agreed having already been provided an extravagant quote a few months prior by an Australian company who later I learned simply outsourced coding to Indian IT companies, and two weeks later sent the plans for the app to his office.

In August, I decided to visit India to sit beside the developers as opposed to our regular Skype calls. Despite the airline's questionable safety record (it had crashed twice recently), a half-price business class ticket was too tempting to resist. Only four passengers occupied the business section—a fact that even made me nervous.

Flying over Mumbai's slums, I was stunned. Blue tarpaulins stretched across hillsides, and millions of people survived below. How lucky I felt.

Machine guns greeted me at the regional airport. Beyond them, a landscape of dusty dilapidated houses, some just plastic bag tents, and stray farm animals stretched out. I felt overwhelmed, wondering if I should have just stayed on Skype.

The IT company was impressive—five floors of specialized staff. Android developers, web services, iOS teams, all working in focused rows. Their education, competence, and courtesy impressed me deeply.

My days became a rhythm of meetings, progress reports, and evening meals of chicken tikka. I was developing something more than an app. I was finding a purpose beyond my cosmetic supply business.

"Your app could help millions," Kuldeep said during one of our meetings in Indore, knowing a little of my story. "People struggling with the same demons you're fighting."

He didn't know how deeply those words would cut. How they would become a mirror, reflecting my own journey of survival.

Each line of code became an act of self-preservation. Each feature is a step toward understanding my own fragmented self. I wasn't just developing an app. I was developing myself as I'd realise in time.

•●•

The mountain seemed to lean in closer. Jonas had grown quite—unusually so. Where previous days had been filled with probing questions, now only silence accompanied our climb.

Revelations began pouring into my consciousness with each step upwards balancing on loose scree with emptiness below the cliff faces next to my boots: There is no final outcome. Pushing forward is the goal and reward. Always fall forward.

Tears emerged—not from sadness, but from a profound recognition. Personal development isn't about reaching a perfect state. It's about continuous movement. About refusing to stay broken.

"The app was my real try at healing," I said to Jonas, my voice breaking. "Not just for other people. For myself, but I didn't know it at the time. Only years later. I'd wake early before the kids in my custody week and work on the app with absolute passion and dedication. It gave me an outlet for my pain and disillusionment about not owning my business anymore. I had to know there was hope for me to become successful again."

He nodded with a spark of comprehension in his eyes. "We heal ourselves by opening up pathways for others to heal."

The summit seemed nearer. Not only a physical peak, but a symbolic change— each step a conscious act of becoming.

Tears of joy started flowing. Proof that my journey was right.

But when the app started, my desperate plunge into self-development began. Years later and after that first suicide contemplation when Michaela left, I knew my brain needed rewiring. Not just an adjustment—a complete reconstruction. I couldn't survive another day in the same mental space that had consumed me during some period's years prior. The constant pain was too great, and I had no choice left but to grow out of my current limitations.

"I totally binge-learned," I told Jonas. "Twenty-four hours a day, no time for distractions. I'd listen to podcasts in the car, at work, even at night when I slept."

Jonas's eyebrow rose. "While you were asleep?"

"I figured if there was even a chance that my brain could learn something positive even subconsciously, I had to try. I was devouring development material, constantly taking courses, studying psychology on apps, anything that would rebuild what had broken inside of me."

Its obsessiveness was easy to justify—I'd go from one form of content to another without pause in between, trying to make every waking and sleeping moment productive—not for entertainment but for survival.

"That intense reprogramming directly resulted in the Christmas Day windsurfing marathon," I went on. "Two and a half weeks after almost ending it all, I somehow managed to windsurf 424 kilometres in less than ten hours."

Jonas whistled softly.

"Physically, I was shattered but could have kept sailing if the wind kept blowing—my muscles drained by weeks of emotional destruction. But my mind was now stronger than my body. When I was out on the water, something inside first whispered: 'Stay out here. This is your world now. Nothing is waiting for you on shore.' So, I did. Sailing and jibing back and forth in Albany's flat waters hundreds of times.

It was around the 310 km mark when my inner voice changed. It started to contemplate a new life—one without my dear Michaela. "You'll meet someone new. Traveling will be simple, and the kids may return." The universe somehow aligned, the wind steadied, and I could linger in these thoughts, imagining what this life might look like. It wasn't joyful, but it was possible. Not happiness, not yet, but feelings I could begin to entertain. There was a pause, a waiting period before strength returned, before I could grasp the fulfilled life I had once promised my younger self.

As the kilometres stretched on and the sun dipped behind the hills, silhouetted by the sail, the wind began to lessen. There was more strength in me, and I wasn't ready to stop. I didn't want to be forced to retire while I could still push forward. Despite my fleeting acceptance of a future, the thought of stepping onto land alone—no Michaela, no Luke, no Olivia—was crushing. And once again the realization woke me that I wasn't ready to face that silence. The past weeks without Michaela had been unbearable, let alone the recent times without the natural closeness of my children. I was willing to trade emotional pain for physical strain if it meant delaying that moment just a little longer.

The horizon stretched endlessly as 400 km ticked over. My muscles ached, and my skin was encrusted with salt where sweat and spray had dried. Dusk crept in, and the wind, as if hearing my unspoken plea, surged one last time. One final gift of time to contemplate my new life before forcing me back to shore. And so, as the wind died and I slowly sailed toward the shore, I prepared to face life on land again, uncertain but still standing.

"If it hadn't been for that psychological reconditioning," I realized, "I wouldn't have made it to the beach at all, let alone endured out there for almost ten hours." My subconscious had carried me forward long after my body wished to stop. I had abandoned the old me—the alcoholic, the gambler, the man consumed by his own destruction.

I thought, "Trust your instincts." Don't chase something for the sake of it. The journey will guide your direction. Have faith in yourself.

10

LET LOVE IN AGAIN

Learning to risk the heart again after devastation

The air felt light, my lungs working hard to extract enough oxygen to keep up with my racing pulse as Jonas and I reached the summit. After three days of climbing, pushing through physical and emotional barriers, we stood atop the peak that had beckoned me since my arrival in New Zealand.

I surveyed the panorama that had once represented my family's future—emerald valleys, sapphire lakes, towering mountains. A landscape that promised the simplicity, connection, and healing I had dreamed of giving Luke and Olivia.

Now, fifteen years later, I stood tracing with my eyes the paths they might have taken had that vision come to life. I wondered what kind of relationship I might have had with my children if we'd grown together in this quiet place. Would the rhythm of country life have softened our edges, drawn us closer?

I often asked myself: would the space, the stillness, have offered me a chance to step out from under the stress of business and face the shadows of my past more gently? And perhaps… would it have offered Dianne something too? A chance to grow into contentment. To discover peace not in control or constant motion, but in presence. In the quiet gift of family, just as it was.

The wind whipped at my white shirt, carrying the bite of ice and distant rain as these questions faded. Answers were irrelevant but asked as if they were expelled. An unwanted residual distraction to the beauty and opportunity surrounding me. Below us, the beautiful distant valley stretched in a tapestry of green pastures and lakes reflecting the shifting clouds above.

"We made it," I breathed, my voice barely audible over the wind's steady roar.

Jonas smiled, his weathered face brightening as he surveyed the panorama. "Third time's the charm."

I planted my feet firmly on the rock, feeling the mountain's solid presence beneath me. Something about standing here, after days of struggle and revelation, brought a clarity I hadn't expected. Not triumph, not conquest, but a quiet understanding that settled inside me.

"Beautiful, isn't it?" Jonas gestured toward the vista. "Worth every step."

I nodded, unable to form words around the tightness in my throat. The summit itself was far smaller than I'd imagined—just a few square meters of rocky terrain—but the view was boundless, stretching to horizons I hadn't known existed before this climb.

"You know," Jonas said, settling onto a small flat rock positioned on a loose scree, "mountains teach us something about love."

I turned to face him, raising an eyebrow. "How's that?"

"Both require you to be vulnerable. To risk pain for the possibility of something extraordinary." He pulled a battered water bottle from his pack. "Both demand that you keep going when every instinct tells you to turn back."

The words struck me with unexpected force. For months after the separation from my ex-wife, I'd guarded my heart with vigilance, building walls no one could breach. The idea of opening myself to that kind of pain again had seemed not just foolish, but dangerous.

Until Michaela.

"Five months after the separation," I told Jonas, gazing into the horizon, "I met someone who changed everything."

The memory surfaced with startling clarity—not dulled by time but sharpened, each detail preserved and etched in my mind.

---------------------•●•---------------------

Five months after the separation text that shattered my world, I found myself scrolling through dating profiles with the strange detachment of someone flipping through a catalogue from another life. Online dating was foreign territory—something traditional people like me didn't do. Most fathers with broken marriages didn't get second chances at love. At least, that's what I told myself thinking my father had just been lucky a few years after separating from my mum to find new love. But I was curious. Could life still offer me another opportunity?

Then I saw her profile. Michaela. Something in her eyes caught me—a warmth that seemed to reach through the screen and touch something I thought had died the day Dianne drove away. My hand held the mouse; my finger hovered over the button. What was I doing? I was barely keeping my head above water—managing the business, handling custody arrangements, trying not to fall apart in front of Luke and Olivia. The last thing I needed was more complication.

But I clicked "like" anyway. What did I have to lose? I had already lost everything.

Michaela reached out in a way that was both beautiful and friendly. We swapped intimate details about our lives, and something about our connection felt immediate. It was meant to be. That feeling led us to arrange a meeting for a drink—to talk in person, to see if the energy we felt through the app was real.

We arranged to meet at a bar in an apartment where I was staying. I nervously checked my phone, half-hoping she'd cancel so I could retreat to the safety of my controlled, compartmentalized grief. "I'm here" Michaela had texted.

When I saw Michaela arrive, walking toward me over the bridge from the carpark from a distance, I felt it again. She was stunning—elegant, stylish, smiling. A warm glow sparked in my chest, and I knew I was falling in love. I didn't need to learn much more about her. Our conversations had already told me everything that mattered—she was loyal, having nursed her ex-husband through cancer, family-oriented, and a wonderful mother to her beautiful boys. As she came closer, I was sure she saw my beaming smile welcoming her into my life.

I stood, awkward and too aware of myself. "Michaela?"

"Mark," she smiled, extending her hand. Her voice was softer than I'd expected, confident and warm. Her blond hair framed a warm, open face that seemed to radiate genuineness. "I was worried I'd be late. Traffic was a nightmare."

We walked together into the dimly-lit bar and each ordered an espresso martini and connected strongly with genuine conversation that allowed us to study each other without being obvious about it. Then she mentioned her boys—thirteen and fifteen—and asked about my kids. Describing Luke and Olivia with pride, she leaned forward. "Mine are with their dad this week. Those first nights of quiet nearly broke me."

Just like that, the careful script of first-date conversation fell away. "Yes," I breathed, relief washing through me at being truly seen. "Exactly that."

That night, we shared another espresso martini and talked for hours, sitting close, wrapped in conversation. I could feel her energy—effortless, comforting. She made me happy, a new type of feeling and different to what I'd previously experienced. A happiness that radiated contemplating a wonderful future with Michaela.

I knew it that night—Michaela and I would become close, our lives intertwining in ways I couldn't yet imagine. Who would have thought that in the midst of such tragic circumstances, love could be found in the rubble of what my life had become?

We promised each other that night that we would meet again. And we did.

And that became the most wonderful relationship I could have ever imagined.

———————————•●•———————————

"The relationship grew passionately and quickly," I told Jonas as we stood atop the mountain. "Weekly coffees became dinners, became weekends together when Luke and Olivia were with Dianne. Michaela had two boys of her own, so she understood the complexities, the constant navigating of schedules and boundaries."

"What made her so special?" Jonas asked, his gaze steady.

I considered this, searching for the right words. "She accepted me. Didn't expect me to hide my pain or pretend to be whole. She just loved me. I could feel it every time she'd speak to me or was around me...Her love radiated constantly towards me.

The wind gusted, bringing the scent of imminent rain. Below us, clouds cast shifting shadows across the valley.

"Eight years together," I continued. "Eight years of rebuilding, of learning to trust again, of believing I could still have some version of the life I'd dreamed of."

Jonas nodded, encouraging me to continue.

———————————•●•———————————

Our love soon fell into its routine, dictated by the custody schedule that controlled both our lives. We spent one week together, wrapped up in each other, and then one week apart, each caring for our children in our separate houses.

During our weeks together, we'd count the hours till we met at her place or mine, and dance to music from our youth as we prepared elaborate dinners or enjoyed our favourite steak, red wine, and salt and vinegar chips Michaela relished so much. Saturdays were morning trips to farmers markets, walks along the river, and picnics as the weather allowed. Sunday nights we'd watch a film cuddled up on the couch, savouring those final hours before we parted once more first thing Monday morning.

"Where were you twenty years ago?" was our mantra, whispered to each other in quiet moments as we'd laugh over red wine while talking of the future. "I would have had children with you," she'd say, and I would concur, attempting to reconcile what would have been had we met before all of that—before failed marriages before children we now shared between two houses. Michaela was the perfect example of what had eluded me in marriage. She possessed every characteristic I could wish for in a lifelong partner.

Yet there was a beauty in this as well—the never-ending reunion, the joy of expectation. Being apart stopped us from getting used to each other. Each fortnightly reunion was like falling in love again.

—·•●•·—

"She had the boys, and I had Luke and Olivia," I explained to Jonas, "and we coped. We were together every week the kids were with their other parents. It was like being eighteen again—all that passion, that sense that everything meant so much."

We lived five years in this cadence, content with our weeks on and then separated when we'd have our kids. Both wounded from past relationships, we were determined to get it right this time, believing we finally had.

"We were soulmates," I told him bluntly. "The kind of connection people spend their whole lives searching for."

We went away one weekend down south to a quint farm property. A base to tour the vineyards and retire back to the cozy couch and fireplace. It was all planned by me. Even an engagement ring was ready to propose.

It was a wonderful afternoon galivanting amongst the wineries. Michaela was radiant in her pink top and black textured scarf, her blond curls catching the late afternoon light as we clinked glasses of golden wine. Her warmth and radiant smile were so beautiful. They confirmed what I was about to do: ask her to be my wife until the end of our time.

On our return, we strolled across the vibrant green lawn that stretched out before us, the grass so lush it seemed to glow in the fading light. The property opened to a breathtaking view—shimmering water in the distance reflecting the sky, bordered by a gentle line of eucalyptus trees that swayed slightly in the breeze. Michaela was out the back admiring the green paddocks and sheep grazing amongst the gum trees and green pastures.

I adjusted my navy sweater nervously, the weight of the moment making my heartbeat visible beneath the blue checkered shirt I wore underneath. The silver watch on my wrist caught the light as I approached her. Walking up to her from behind, I tapped her to notice my falling to my knee.

"Will you marry me," I said, the words tumbling out. Her eyes opened wide, searching my face. A long pause ensued just long enough for me to ask myself if she was indeed wanting.

And then she clutched my hand, her delicate fingers adorned with a simple ring. Her eyes reflected both our faces against the backdrop of the stunning landscape, glistening with tears. "Yes. Of course, yes."

We sealed the promise with a kiss, our foreheads touching tenderly, smiling so wide our cheeks ached, the sprawling countryside a silent witness to our moment. We ended the day talking of houses we would own, holidays we would have, and a future that was suddenly, blissfully real.

For a time, that promise was sufficient.

———————— •●•————————

"But as time passed, things got complicated," I said. "Every time her boys came over to visit their mum, I saw what I was missing with my own children."

Luke was slipping away—first in subtle ways, then all at once. He stopped coming over during my custody weeks, and slowly, his replies to my messages faded into silence. Weeks became months, then the absence became complete: nine months without a single word or explanation. Olivia followed a similar path. Her once-bright voice messages became shorter, more reserved—until one day, they stopped altogether. Six months passed in quiet. I knew they were both hurting, carrying pain of their own, but I couldn't reach them. I couldn't comfort them. I couldn't find the words to bridge the growing space between us.

Meanwhile, Michaela's boys became constant fixtures in my life—celebrating birthdays, sharing dinners, flopping on the couch after their mum's dinners. Their laughter and energy filled the house with a familiar rhythm I craved. They were good kids—bright, respectful, warm. But with every "thanks for dinner", or story about their week, something inside me twisted.

"What really got to me," I told Jonas, was the silence around Luke and Olivia. We'd be at the dinner table, Michaela's boys chatting away about school and sports, and no one would mention my kids. Not out of cruelty—just absence. As if they'd vanished from the narrative."

Michaela was always kind, always encouraging me to reach out, to invite Luke and Olivia. And I did. I tried. But their absence made each experience harder to enjoy.

I did my best to stay present—to smile, to ask Michaela's boys about their studies, their friendships, their dreams. I wanted to be welcoming, not resentful. But inside, I was severely haemorrhaging.

The more present her sons became, the more acutely I felt the absence of mine. It wasn't anyone's fault—not theirs, not Michaela's, not Luke's or Olivia's. It was just the nature of loss when there's no clear ending. A wound without a funeral. A grief that left no space for closure.

I picked up a small stone, turning it over in my palm. "One night, after Michaela's boys had been over, I sat alone in my study, looking through old photos of Luke and Olivia.

The contrast was too painful. Michaela's easy, healthy rhythm with her children illuminated the growing distance between me and mine. It cast a sharp light on what I had lost—and what I hadn't been able to repair.

A quiet kind of sadness took hold of me. Not dramatic, just heavy. I felt worn down by the ache, ashamed that my grief could feel so consuming. But it did. Gradually, it weakened me. And eventually, I found myself unable to cope."

———————————•●•———————————

Rain lashed against the windows as I sat in darkness, the glow from my laptop casting harsh shadows across the room. On-screen, photos from happier times— Luke's tenth birthday, Olivia's ballet recital, and family holidays before everything fell apart.

Michaela's laughter drifted up from downstairs, her younger son's voice rising in protest at whatever his mum's comments would be. The easy affection in their conversations was a knife twisting in my gut.

I closed the laptop, plunging the room into darkness that matched my mood. My chest felt hollow, scraped raw with longing. With her kindness and patience, this beautiful woman downstairs deserved someone who could fully embrace her life with her boys—not a man constantly haunted by what he'd lost.

When she found me later, I couldn't see her eyes.

"Talk to me," she said, settling beside me on the edge of the bed. "What's going on?"

"I can't do this anymore," I whispered, the words tearing from me.

Her hand stilled on my shoulder. "Do what?"

"They're slipping away from me, Michaela. Every day, a little more."

She was silent for a long moment, her breathing steady beside me. When she finally spoke, her voice was gentle but resolute. "You're not failing. You're navigating an impossible situation with as much grace as anyone could."

"I don't feel graceful," I said bitterly. "I feel broken beyond repair."

"Then be broken," she said simply. "But don't push me away because of it."

I looked at her then, this woman who had walked through the wasteland of my grief without flinching. Who had shown me it was possible to build something meaningful from the rubble.

"I don't know how to separate my love for you from my grief over them," I admitted. "The two are so tangled I can't tell where one ends and the other begins."

She took my hand, her touch an anchor in the storm. "Then don't try. Just feel it all—the love, the grief, the anger. I'm not going anywhere."

But even as she said it, I felt a shift inside me. As if something had already begun to let go. The darkness was pulling at me again, and I was too tired—too hollowed out—to fight it. Not anymore.

— • ● • —

"I pushed her away," I told Jonas, the regret thick in my voice. "Not all at once—but slowly, almost imperceptibly. I began withdrawing emotionally, creating distance where there had once been connection. I became critical, frustrated that she couldn't fully see how much it hurt to have her sons filling the space where my children used to be."

153

I paused, swallowing hard. "I told myself she deserved better than what I could offer. And maybe she did. But it wasn't just that—I was afraid. Afraid of more loss. Afraid that building a future with someone else's kids while being estranged from my own would break me completely."

"It wasn't all conscious," I added. "My tone, my body language, the distorted way I heard her words… they were all shaped by years of unresolved grief. I thought I was being noble, stepping back to avoid hurting her. But really, I was protecting myself—from feeling more pain than I could carry."

"I was in agony over the separation from my kids. And being in my home filled with someone else's children at times, no matter how kind they were, made me feel like I was betraying something deep in my DNA. It wasn't their fault. Or hers. But I couldn't imagine going to another milestone event like an 18th or 21st birthday, meeting someone else's first partner, celebrating occasions that weren't my children's. The thought felt like slow death."

"My ambition to build a beautiful life with Michaela faded under the weight of that grief. It's not that I didn't love her. I did. But the pain had taken over. And I was drowning in it."

It was around then that Michaela and I began to talk seriously about marriage. She wanted to own part of the house she lived in. I understood—she wanted to feel secure. To build something with me on equal ground.

"I'll sell mine too," she promised. "Once yours sells."

Mine sold quickly, and I was eager for Michaela to follow. We had a 12-month lease-back period to make our next move. But the pressure of a new business, financial strain, and the emotional weight of selling the home that had once held my hopes for me, my kids and a future with Michaela were beginning to take their toll.

One evening, after a particularly exhausting day, I asked Michaela gently when she planned to list her home.

"I'll do it when I'm ready," she said. Her voice was sharper than I expected. "Stop pressuring me!"

I sat there, stunned. All the sacrifices I'd made, the generosity I'd extended—especially around welcoming her kids into our life in my home while mine remained absent—rose in my throat like bile. I felt something shift inside me. Not rage, but exhaustion. A deep, soul-tired ache.

I carried the heaviness to Olivia's old bedroom, a space I had held sacred. I sat in the dark, unsure of what I was feeling—resentment, guilt, betrayal, grief. I felt disloyal to my own DNA. I'd tried to love Michaela and her sons wholeheartedly, but somewhere inside, a quiet voice kept asking: What about your own children? What would Luke think, knowing you're giving your energy to someone else's family while he stays silent?

To Michaela's credit, she came downstairs and sat beside me. Her voice was soft, full of concern. "I'm sorry, Mark, for how I reacted," she said. "Let's try to make the best of this weekend."

But something had cracked. My emotional skin felt sunburned, too raw to endure another brush of discomfort. I woke the next morning wondering: Is this the rest of my life? Watching someone else's children arrive to my home, while mine won't even return my calls?

The pressure of my business, the silence from Luke and Olivia, the man who had refused to meet me yet lived with my kids, the bright-eyed conversations at our dinner table from sons who weren't mine—all of it accumulated like lead in my bones.

The following morning I signed the settlement documents, my hand shaking with indecision. But I didn't go home to Michaela. I couldn't. I couldn't face her bright talk of wedding plans while I felt so disoriented and hollow.

I drove aimlessly, street names blurring, until I stopped in front of a brothel. I didn't go there out of desire. I went there out of pure, undeniable destruction.

A voice inside me—clearer than any I'd heard in months—whispered: Mark, this is killing you. You can't keep pretending. You're not surviving. You're drowning.

I parked. I walked in. Not as a man seeking pleasure, but as someone desperate to sabotage what little good remained—because I didn't feel worthy of it anymore.

When I got home that night, Michaela asked where I'd been. Her voice held suspicion, but not accusation.

"Yes," I said. "I went in."

She didn't cry. She didn't scream. She just said, quietly but with finality: "You've just ruined your life." My life was already ruined I thought, and my act just confirmed what I felt. Michaela just didn't understand it though my long suppression of emotions. Then, she turned upstairs, packed a bag, and left.

The door slammed with a kind of silence that echoed through the house long after she was gone.

I stood in the hallway, too hollow to cry. I'd sabotaged the one beautiful thing left in my life—not because I didn't love Michaela, but because I could no longer carry the weight of watching someone else's family flourish in the shadow of my own grief.

I was too ashamed to admit the truth: that I was jealous, overwhelmed, and completely broken by the ongoing absence of my own children.

I wished I'd had the courage to say what I really needed. That I needed space. That I needed time. That I needed Michaela to understand my grief not as rejection, but as pain I was still learning to carry. Something still to process.

I think Michaela would have listened. She might not have understood it fully, but she would have tried. Because she loved me.

But I didn't speak. I collapsed instead.

"Fear makes us do terrible things to the people we love," Jonas observed, his voice gentle.

"I've learned something fundamental through all this," I told Jonas, my voice steady despite the emotion welling in my chest. "Loving someone allows you to love yourself. When you put energy into enhancing yourself and another person, something magical happens—one plus one doesn't equal two. It equals three."

Jonas nodded his weathered face thoughtful in the mountain light. "Creation from connection."

"Exactly. For months after the marriage separation, I tried to protect my heart, building fortresses against further pain. But those same walls that kept hurt out also kept healing at bay." I gestured toward the valley spread beneath us. "Like refusing to climb this mountain because you might fall."

"And now?" Jonas asked.

"Now I understand that we don't heal in isolation. We heal through connection—through opening ourselves to joy at the risk of pain." I gazed out into the distance. "The heart isn't meant to be a fortress. It's meant to be a bridge to let love in and out. It has to breathe too, or it suffocates."

A sudden gust of wind cut across the peak, sharp and cold against my skin. I closed my eyes and let it pass through me, anchoring myself to the solidity of the mountain beneath my feet. Memories rose and fell behind my eyelids—moments of joy, loss, regret, and resilience—blending into a quiet storm of reflection. I stood still, tracing the path of emotions that had carried me here. When I opened my eyes again, something within me had shifted. It wasn't dramatic, just deeply certain—a quiet sense of wholeness, as if a long-fractured part of me had quietly, finally, come home.

"Don't protect your heart," I said quietly. "Open it to heal with someone new. That's the lesson I had to learn the hardest way possible. The opposite of love to me was complete loneliness in isolation and pain."

———————————— •●• ————————————

I wanted to love again. Soon after Michaela left, I had learned in self-development that if you want to resolve an area of pain in life, focus on improving that area. Don't focus valuable energy on something else unrelated. So, I had a failing relationship. I set about having a positive relationship.

A few months after Michaela left, I met a woman named Isabella. We connected online and agreed to meet for a drink at a hotel. I sat at a table where I could watch the entrance, curious whether her photos would match the woman in real life.

When an Uber pulled up, I looked up casually—then froze. A tall, striking woman with long, wavy dark hair stepped out, an Italian lady with model elegance and confidence to match. I was so struck I forgot I was waiting for a date.

"Hello, Mark," she said with a warm smile, approaching with surety. I paused and smiled as I stood up to hold her extended hand in welcome. "Hello, Isabella," I said, indicating an available seat at the small table.

We sat and began exchanging introductions. Then she said, without hesitation, "I don't do drugs—and I'm not into people who do."

"Neither do I," I replied a little shocked but confidently. And then I paused, realising the truth beneath my answer. I was a reformed alcoholic.

Isabella captivated me—not just her beauty, but her vibrant energy. As we spoke, we discovered a shared pain: an acrimonious separation. When she realised I, too, suffered from the same situation, she began to cry.

"I can't believe someone else understands," she whispered, tears streaming down her face.

One glass of wine became two, then three. Her tone grew louder, her body language more emphatic. I knew the signs. Wine was no longer just a drink—it was in charge. I had walked this path before.

Despite the warning bells, I wanted to see her again. But I knew then: I couldn't fall deeply. Alcohol would always come first unless she confronted it. I saw the signs of what I had lived and nearly lost everything to. I couldn't pretend not to see them in her.

We kept dating. There were joyful moments—her humour, her drive, our conversations that stretched into early morning. But the wine never stopped flowing. I would quietly stop at two glasses. She would keep going.

I opened up to her one night. "I've struggled with alcohol in the past," I said gently. "That's why I stop when I do."

"That's a shame," she replied, sipping her glass. "A wine with dinner is fine."

Sometimes she'd share stories of childhood issues, marriage heartbreak, of her ongoing pain. Her tears would flow freely after enough wine. And with time, so did her rage. One night, I drove her home after she lashed out during an argument I never intended.

The cycle repeated—alcohol, tears, accusations, and silence. The next day, warm texts would arrive like nothing had happened. I loved her sober self. But every bottle reopened her wounds and mine.

Isabella was energetic—fit and active and trading the share market. We spoke about my business, our hopes, and past lives. Her options trading reminded me of my own addiction to the share market post-divorce, chasing what I'd lost. I saw that same blind chase in her.

Our last evening together ended with her shouting, tears streaking her face. "You have no empathy!" she cried. "You don't care about my pain!"

I'd spent dozens of nights comforting her, holding her through sobs. But this time, my compassion met a wall. "The drinking is making this worse, Isabella," I said gently. "This isn't you talking."

I left quietly as her words followed me out the door. I'd walked this path before, and I knew: I couldn't fix her. She had to choose her own healing.

For weeks, I found myself missing her—talking to her memory as if she were still beside me. Her wit, her warmth, her active mind. I wished she'd take that first step toward healing. But she didn't.

Over time, I realised I had also fallen short. I had hoped she would follow me on the recovery path without ever asking if she was ready. I was impatient. I wanted her to catch up and join me in healing. But healing isn't forced. It's chosen.

"I can't save you," I whispered to her memory one night. "You have to want to save yourself."

I came to see that love, even when it's real, can't thrive where addiction is unacknowledged. And that no matter how much good is present, addiction makes a terrible master.

I still believe in a healthy relationship with alcohol. These days, it's a glass of red paired with a flame-grilled New Zealand scotch fillet—medium rare, fat rendered just right. That's all it needs to be. Not a crutch. Not a wound duller. Just flavour.

I had loved again after Michaela. And I had learned. Unacknowledged addiction will always win until it's named, owned, and faced. And love can't thrive when its roots grow beside denial.

———————————— •●• ————————————

I hadn't listened to my heart—not when it came to the aching absence of my children, and not when its final desperate pulse tried to save me. When we ignore the heart long enough, it acts out in desperation. Mine had resorted to extreme measures—not to destroy me, but to survive. Its final cry was that afternoon I drove to a brothel. It wasn't about Michaela. It wasn't about betrayal. It was a self-inflicted rupture—a plea to end the agony I could no longer articulate.

I knew it was the *situation*, not Michaela, which was killing my heart. But in trying to end that pain, I caused enormous damage to someone I deeply cared for. Michaela—beautiful, kind, undeserving—was caught in the crossfire of a soul on fire. I used silence to shield her from my inner torment, quietly weeping in bed beside her, hoping she wouldn't hear me or feel my wet pillow as she'd roll to hug me. I didn't want to poison our time together with my sadness or show her the depth of my weakness.

I turned to share this with Jonas—one last insight.

But he was gone.

No footsteps. No sound. Just absence.

I stood up suddenly, my heart thudding. "Jonas!" I yelled out, voice slicing the crisp air, echoing across the cliffs, only to be swallowed by the silence.

Had he fallen?

Had I drifted too far inside my own thoughts, missing the moment he slipped away?

I turned in slow circles, the vast emptiness of the summit wrapping itself around me. The same summit we had reached together—Jonas and I. The same mountain that had held me through three days of confession, memory, and pain. Now it was only me. Alone. Or perhaps, not quite.

I knelt slowly onto a smooth granite rock, just a step from the edge. My knees folded beneath me as if in surrender, and I gazed down at the familiar small stones beneath my boots. Then slowly, I lifted my eyes to the sky—endless, patches of clear, dark clouds and blue—stretching above the towering peaks of New Zealand's South Island Alps.

This was my Nirvana.

The place I had always dreamed of bringing my family.

The place I thought would host us all.

But it was here, alone on this mountaintop, that I was finally being healed.

The chilly air bit at my skin, but it awakened something deep in me. A clarity. A stillness. The frantic noise of the past ten years—the pain, the grief, the guilt—began to settle like snow, soft and silent. beneath it, I felt something unexpected stirring:

Love. For Luke. For Olivia. For myself.

Then it came—the understanding I hadn't dared to name until now.

There was something about Jonas—always had been. A strange, familiar knowing in his eyes. A softness that wasn't quite earthly. The way he listened to my story as if he already knew every line. As if he had lived it with me.

I reached into my pack, pulling out my wallet with shaking hands. I unfolded the creased photograph.

The boy stared back—six years old, bright-eyed, smiling standing next to his tall wooden tower.

The boy I once made a promise to in my home office, years ago, when I was ready to give up. The boy with Jonas's face.

And in that moment, the mountain, the silence, the pain—they all fell away.

"It was you," I whispered, breath catching. "It was always you."

Jonas hadn't been a hiker. He hadn't been real—not in the way I first believed.

He was *me*. He was my younger self. My innocence. My heart. The young boy I promised ten years ago of the life he deserved.

He had walked me up this mountain to remind me of who I once was. Who I still am beneath the scars. His quiet presence had been my lifeline, his eyes the mirror of a soul begging me to live.

"Don't die, Dad." His message ten years ago. His plea. His love.

The tears came, full and free, cutting warm paths down my cold cheeks. They weren't just tears of pain—but of release. Of grace. Of return.

The mountain had listened. It had held me through my darkest memories, my regrets, my shame. And now, it gave me back to myself.

I was still a father. A father worthy of love. A father *capable* of love. And that was enough.

The tears kept coming, unclogging the hardened riverbeds in my soul where love had been dammed too long. I felt it rush toward Luke and Olivia—unfiltered, unburdened by the past. I felt it flow inward, too, toward the man who had survived. Toward the little boy who had never stopped believing we'd come home.

There, high above the world, the wind wrapped around me like a blessing.

And for the first time in years, I felt it:

Peace. Forgiveness. The beginning of a new kind of love. I looked out over the horizon—my Nirvana stretched out before me, vast and luminous.

This was not the future I once imagined. It was something better. Because it was real.

And now, with an open heart and clearer eyes, I was ready to be their father again—however that might look.

11

THE WHITE LIGHT DREAM

A profound realisation about survival and inner purpose

I lay in a new type of solitude that night in my hotel room. I felt a comfort I hadn't felt previously in separation. Physical exhaustion had met an emotional settling. The pieces of trauma Jonas had pried open with his questioning seemed processed unlike before. Issues that once caused agitation no longer triggered the same physical response. My eyes closed heavily, settling my muscles and relaxing into repair as I drifted out of consciousness. The ceiling disappeared, replaced by a warm darkness punctuated by fragments of memory—my children's laughter, the mountain's whispers, Jonas's knowing eyes. Three days of revelations with Jonas and a lifetime of traumas preceding a forced separation from my kids had taken their toll when finally, I could start to heal.

Shattered, I drifted for a moment recalling hugging my kids one summer night after swimming in our family home pool fifteen years ago. Squeals of delight sounded as I would launch Olivia into the air, pausing just before she splashed into the glowing floodlit water. Luke crawled on the pool ledge then jumped in with a loud, "Woohoo!" A happy memory sent me off to deep slumber.

———————————•●•———————————

A blinding white light pulsed behind my eyelids, expanding and contracting like a living thing. I stood on a mountain trail I did not recognize when I opened my eyes. Had I always been here? I couldn't remember arriving, yet the path stretched ahead as if waiting for me. The ground beneath my feet felt strange—not the jagged, uneven rock I expected, but something smoother, almost polished as if the earth itself had been reshaped.

The air shimmered, each breath unnaturally crisp, filling my lungs with an unsettling clarity. The colours around me were too vivid, sharper than reality should allow. Something in me whispered that none of this was real. That I was somewhere else—somewhere in between.

Then Jonas appeared beside me, wearing the same worn green jacket, yet somehow newer, untouched by time. His presence had the unmistakable clarity that only dream figures possess—more vibrant and essential than their waking counterparts.

"Your wealth isn't what you think or wish it is," Jonas said.

He'd appeared beside me, as the trail in front of us wound its way through impossibly green alpine meadows where there hadn't been any path.

"What wealth?" I responded. "I did not come here in search of anything tangible."

Jonas smiled, that uncomfortably knowing smile. "Wealth is never material, Mark. Where your heart is, that's where you'll find it. You have to discover your wealth so the journey you've been on for the past ten years will be worthwhile—so all these lessons will make sense."

We walked beside a brook that hadn't existed seconds earlier, water gurgling over rocks that shone like glass.

"You returned to New Zealand to discover yourself, how life may unfold," he went on. "The green light you were seeking was there all the time, waiting patiently for you to see it."

The trail rose steadily, threading its way among rocks that sparkled with minerals I couldn't identify. "How will I recognize it when I see it?" I asked.

"Your heart will lead you to your wealth," Jonas told me. "And signs of significant events of the past ten years will remind you along the way. They come in terms that you will understand if you're listening."

"You'll attempt to tune them out at first. You may not recognize what they are," he went on. "But just like my voice telling you to get help, to find your tribe, to remove addictions, look after your body, and to find love, my voice will grow louder until you feel restless, uneasy in your own skin. You heard me during the two times you were about to give up on your life and mine. You'll question whether you should've abandoned your old self earlier. What held you back so long was fear— fear that if you left, you'd never come back. But you'll always be a father."

The trail narrowed and pushed me toward the face of the mountain. "I'm not afraid anymore."

The words left my mouth with a conviction I hadn't felt in years. And strangely, I realized they were true. The fear that had been my constant companion—of irrelevance, of failing my children, of disappointing my younger self—had begun to loosen its grip.

"Aren't you?" Jonas gave me a knowing look. "If you choose to ignore your significant life events, their meaning will abandon you because you stopped listening to them. Their silent effect on you will indicate to you your wealth is concealed forever. You can become wealthy in money, but you'll spend every day knowing you didn't follow your life path to find your true wealth. And now it's beyond the point of no return when you'll live a regretful life unfulfilled."

Wind swept across the trail, carrying the scent of distant rain.

"Real love doesn't hinder a man from his own destiny," Jonas began, his voice growing louder and more powerful with each word. "If he veers off his path for another, then it wasn't real love. Make a commitment and move on. Do something. Follow your heart because where your heart is; that's where you'll find your wealth."

The trail twisted, opening out into a landscape I had never known—terrain unfamiliar yet somehow recognizable, as if drawn from the deepest recesses of childhood memory.

"Hear what it has to tell you," he urged. "Your heart will never catch you off guard like it did your father, if you tune in every day. That is how you prevent a crisis."

"And if a crisis comes anyway?" I asked.

"Fear of suffering is worse than suffering itself," Jonas responded. "Time spent deciphering signs of your wealth is a rendezvous with truth. Don't succumb to your fears or you'll never behold your dream."

The sky grew dark, clouds forming with unnatural speed.

"Threats of death remind people to take notice of their lives," Jonas told me, dropping his voice to a whisper. "What kept you alive? Those two times you wanted out. Don't die, Dad. The photo of young Mark you found and promised a better life. Reality. Discipline. Truth."

Lightning flashed far off, illuminating Jonas's face. His features appeared to change for a moment, growing younger and more innocent—more like the boy in the photo I held. In that flicker of recognition, something fundamental clicked into place. The resemblance wasn't coincidental.

"When I battled and was undone, I spoke to you," he said, yet now his voice had changed, younger and yet somehow mine. "So loudly you had to listen."

"What are you saying?" I asked, though half of me already knew the answer.

"Your fate was always to look after that boy in the photo you found—for me," he told me. "The wealth is not out there. It's within."

The earth beneath us began to shimmer, outlines blurring.

"It was me who talked to you," he went on. "To locate me in your adolescence. To find me in your personal items in your home office. I sought assistance when I was shattered, and you received therapy. I was isolated, so I requested that you find love, find your people. It was me who told you 'Don't die, Dad' when you had given up all hope with no children, no Michaela. You had to have heard me. I wanted to live the lovely life you vowed to me all those years ago. I heard your promise."

I dreamt of myself: collapsing outside the respite hospital, two policewomen standing guard over me. The darkness that had surrounded me that day was complete—the first time I'd ever seen such absolute nothingness.

"The little boy deep inside heard my promise from a decade ago," Jonas continued, his voice growing stronger. "He started communicating with me about how to survive—quietly and persistently. You didn't always hear this message consciously. It worked beneath the surface, guiding your actions when you were too broken to see the way forward. Sometimes you were slow to listen, so I had to speak loud at times."

"I spoke to you in moments of decision," he said. "Urging you to seek professional help when pride told you to suffer alone. Reminding you that your children absorb everything and that your demeanour would affect their level of crisis. I whispered about financial stability when gambling beckoned, about strengthening your body when your heart and mind were fractured."

I nodded, understanding implicitly. "All those lessons..."

"Yes," Jonas affirmed. "The push to eliminate dependencies that numbed the pain but arrested progress. The drive to find your tribe—people who shared your passions and could offer friendship when you needed it most. The persistence to keep texting, calling, appearing for your children even when met with silence."

"The courage to open your heart to new love rather than seal it behind walls," I whispered.

"And the commitment to intensive self-development," Jonas added. "Rewiring your brain toward healthy thought patterns. Facing reality head-on instead of hiding in comfortable illusions. Always seeking that white light of hope, no matter how dim, during your darkest hours."

"All along, it was you," I said, my voice thick with emotion. "My younger self, keeping the promise I made to you. You knew I wanted to give you the life you deserved."

Jonas smiled—that innocent, hopeful smile I recognized from the photograph. "We kept it together. I reminded you that healing isn't about justice but accepting the past to create a future. That a heart dies without love. That every lesson was another step toward the life we both deserved."

"I was sick, and I asked you to stop drinking," Jonas continued. "I needed stability, and so you stopped gambling. I am you, Mark. You are me. I will always guide you, but you must always listen."

The mountain path was fading now, reality thinning like morning mist.

"You listen to me, and I'll watch out for you," Jonas vowed. "I'll lead you in the right direction. We're lifelong partners. I didn't want you to go away from me those two times. You must have heard me telling you to get help, to live."

With the melting scenery, I could see his face clearly now—my smiling face from decades earlier standing beside my timber tower before life had drawn its lessons on my skin. The boundaries between us blurred—present and past, adult and child, mentor, and student. We were separate yet one, divided by time yet united in purpose. In this space between worlds, I finally understood what had kept me tethered to life through my darkest moments.

"A small white light appeared," I whispered, understanding its message. "When everything was darkest when I couldn't see a way forward—there was still that tiny spark."

"Yes," said Jonas. "You followed it to this point where you're finally repairing. You did justice to the younger you. You did justice to yourself, and therefore to your children."

The dreamscape had completely dissolved now, and all that was left was Jonas and me, hanging between sleep and wakefulness.

"When you get home," he told me, "You'll be with your daughter. You'll see your son. You'll even hug your ex-wife in front of your daughter. Because you'll realize that guarding your heart by covering it with pride and anger is only causing you more harm."

"Empathy is the antidote," I completed for him.

"Yes. Remember, seeking justice from other humans is a game you can't win. Your opponent is your equal; no victory is possible. Love and empathy are the only answers to peace and survival."

"You will have one final test Mark," Jonas said. "It will determine your future and set your path. You will need every ounce of strength as it will tempt you to unleash all ten years of fury that you've worked to transform."

Jonas—my younger self, my heart—laid a hand on my shoulder. The weight was firm and impossibly gentle.

"Never forget," he whispered as the borders of the dream realm dissolved. "I'm still here. Always." The mountain faded, the light dissolved, and I awoke with my heart still ringing with his voice.

I sat up with a jolt, struck by Jonas's warning—his concern over the final test he said was still to come. The sheet that had been wrapped around my legs fell away, unbound, as my chest heaved with shallow breaths. My heart thundered beneath my ribs. The hotel room was silent, steeped in darkness, except for the soft red glow of the digital clock: Three forty-seven. The same time I'd awakened the night when the first epiphany hit.

But now, instead of panic or confusion, a strange calm settled over me. Not numbness—but something deeper. Peace. Acceptance. A new readiness.

My thoughts reverted to two of the worst moments of my life. The first, the morning after Michaela left me, I'd lay on the pavement outside a respite hospital. I'd rejected going to the main hospital and in doing so also rejected the medications I believed would render me into oblivion.

The second time came just a month later. My friend Tom—steadfast and intuitive—talked me off the ledge of life, quite literally. He called on others from our windsurfing group, forming a small circle of support around me. That day marked the first time I experienced complete and terrifying emotional darkness. Not metaphorically—but quite literally. For a moment, there was no light. The internal flame that had flickered even through the worst of times simply went out. What remained was a cold, calculated logic: I'd lived a full life, and I saw no reason to continue another day.

The Christmas Day windsurfing marathon had briefly lifted me. It had felt like a small, hard-won victory—a declaration that I wasn't defeated. But soon after, the tide turned. The endorphins faded, and the practical burdens of a failed life rushed back in. My new business was under pressure, cashflow was tight, and the dream I had tried to rebuild felt like it was slipping again. I was grieving Michaela and feeling the emotional distance from my kids more than ever. Perth—a city that many years ago felt like a fresh start—now felt like rejection all over again.

That Friday mid-morning, I lay in Olivia's old bedroom, feeling somewhat numb. I had just met with my solicitor to remove Michaela from my Will. My phone buzzed. A message from the settlement agent. "Dear Mr Woodley, congratulations on the settlement of your house…" It should have been good news, but instead, it hit like a sentence. The home I once filled with hope, laughter, and plans for a future with Michaela and my kids now felt like a cell. Michaela had left. Luke's presence in my life had become rare. Olivia's photos remained, but her voice was absent as she had long settled at her mums. And I was now renting what had once been my sanctuary.

I had to leave. To escape the cell, I once owned. But the darkness came with me. Aimlessly, I drove along the river, unsure what to think or where to go. Days earlier, I'd pinned my last hope on a home I'd first tried to buy four years before—a place I believed might finally mark a new beginning. The offer was in, the agent was confident, and for the first time in a long while, I let myself believe in possibility.

Then his number lit up my dashboard. I pressed the talk button, and his voice told me everything. "Mark, I'm sorry. The owner accepted a cash offer." Something broke. Only 4 hours stood between removing Michaela from my Will, the settlement of my house and the collapse of this fragile hope. I drove back to my rental in silence, each turn on the familiar road cutting a little deeper. When I pulled into the driveway—the same spot where, for two and a half years, I'd brought Olivia and Arnie back for our custody weeks and where Michaela had called home—that old ache returned. But now it felt final.

I sat motionless in the car, tears flowing free.

"I'm done," I whispered to no one, yet almost without thinking, I found myself texting Tom—just as I had recently done with Cody.

It wasn't said in panic or drama. It was resignation. After nine years of navigating loss, rejection, courtrooms, grief, and endless starts that never quite took—

something inside me let go. Over 3,200 days had passed since the separation. And here I was: no permanent home, no daily connection with my children, no Michaela, no clear direction. I felt like a ghost still trying to participate in a world that had long moved on.

I climbed the stairs to the bedroom. Michaela's absence echoed louder than ever. I knelt where we'd once embraced countless times, arms wrapping around the air where her body used to lie. I pressed my cheek to where her heart had once beat against mine and whispered goodbye. My thoughts were tangled between the warmth of her, and the memory of my kids as they once were. Was this emotional prison where I truly belonged?

But then Tom arrived. He found me upstairs, unravelled, and empty. And he did something I'll never forget—he stayed. He talked. He listened. He challenged every ounce of my "logic," piece by piece, for hours. He wouldn't let me go quietly. In hindsight, I know I was in the most dangerous place—where despair had become rational. Where death made sense. It wasn't chaos; it was calculation. That's what made it so dangerous.

During my final goodbye to the imagined presence of Michaela, everything went dark. A complete blackness descended—total, consuming, and absolute. There was no panic. Just an eerie calm. No flicker of hope, no desire to continue. I can't say how long I remained in that state. Seconds, maybe minutes. But then, just as I believed I was preparing my plan to slip away for good, a pin-sized white light emerged in the upper right corner of my mind. Faint, almost imperceptible.

It grew slowly.

The light began to take shape—the familiar outline of a photograph I had carried with me for years. A young boy's face. Smiling. Innocent. Full of life. It was young Mark, the boy I had once been—the boy I had made a promise to. To survive. To live a life worthy of him. To give him the future he deserved.

And with that memory, I found the strength to move. I placed my hands on the edge of the bed and pushed myself upright, legs trembling. The dizziness hit immediately, but I held onto the balustrade and made my way downstairs, where Tom—just like Cody before him—had arranged for members of our windsurfing tribe to come and be by my side.

We all gathered in the lounge. The conversation turned again to hospitals, to options, to safety. I listened this time. I wasn't numb or defiant. I was open. I even called James—one of the founding members of our windsurfing team, the man whose vision created the very tribe that saved me. It was through his efforts that I'd met Cody, Tom, and so many others who had shown up when I needed them most. Over the years, I'd come to trust James deeply, often seeking his wisdom in moments of doubt. His quiet leadership had helped create the community that cradled me in my darkest moments.

As we talked, something shifted. In their presence, I began to believe there was another way forward. I still wasn't sold on hospital admission, but I made a promise—to them, and to myself—that I would find a path. I would honour the boy in that photo.

And in doing so, I kept my word—not just to my mates, but to my younger self. I had held on. I had endured. And in that endurance, I had found a form of justice. For myself. For my children. For the life that still lay ahead.

I'd been lying with these thoughts for a few hours. The hotel room was suddenly too tight, the walls closing in. I got dressed hastily and moved outside onto the tiny balcony. The pre-dawn air nipped at me, but I embraced the cutting clarity it provided. Mountains loomed like guards against the still-dark sky; their peaks softened by fading starlight.

I considered what the future held for me at home. I'd hear Olivia laugh, once more. I'd text Luke and keep reaching out with my love, feeling he'd be receptive to a change in me he'd be able to define. I might even, as suggested, hug my ex-wife in front of our daughter—because I was certain that it would help test and define the power of empathy that Jonas has instilled in me and remove my own misery by being bitter.

I'd been crying out for justice for so long—demanding recognition for my suffering, for all that had been taken from me. But Jonas was right: justice at the hands of others is an illusion, a game without winners. The only true path to healing was through empathy—for myself, for my ex-wife, and for my dear children, who had lost their own things too.

For years, I sought justice for the pain of fractured parenting, for the disconnection from my kids, for the loneliness left in the wake of lost relationships. I built walls to protect myself—fortresses of logic, pride, and wounded righteousness—meant to keep the pain out. But those same walls kept healing out too. They trapped me in a cycle of grief and bitterness.

Except for Michaela. With her, somehow, a bridge had been built across the moat. She'd walked over it freely, gently, and with love. And my windsurfing mates—maybe they didn't walk, but I like to think they sailed across it, lifting me out of the waters every time I started to sink.

The earliest light of dawn stretched across the horizon, soft gold brushing the edges of the sky. A new day was beginning. And for the first time in years, I was ready to greet it—not with armour, not with defences, but with an open heart. A quiet knowing had settled over me: my younger self—my truest self—was still with me, guiding me forward.

That small white light—the one that appeared as I prepared for what I thought would be my final moment—had never truly left me. It had travelled faithfully through the shadows, through despair, through silence, and it had led me here. To this mountain. To this awakening.

And now, it was time to carry that light home. Not as a symbol of survival, but as a compass. A steady glow pointing me back to what matters: rebuilding connection with my children. Letting that light illuminate a path I once believed was lost forever.

I watched the sun rise fully over the mountains, golden light spilling cleanly across the ridgelines. I drew in the cold, pure air—steady, whole. I knew the road ahead would be difficult. The scars of the past wouldn't vanish with the morning light. Years of distance, silence, and hurt wouldn't dissolve overnight. But for the first time, I could see beyond the struggle—toward the promise in the distance.

My wealth was not what I once chased. It wasn't the perfect reunion, or the old dream of family restored, or material comfort in a new land. It was this: this stillness. This clarity. This moment of peace with the man I had become. It was the reconciliation with the boy I once was, and the unspoken vow that we would go forward together—no matter what came.

As full daylight bathed the alpine peaks, I made a silent promise:

I will never again silence the voice of my heart. Not when it whispers. Not when it cries out. When I sense a crisis, I will listen—no matter the cost, no matter the discomfort.

Because in that voice lies more than survival. It holds the path to healing. To meaning. To peace. And that—that is a wealth worth any price.

12

PEACE WITHOUT SURRENDER

Healing through quiet acceptance

The hire car clung to the winding mountain highway as I drove back to the airport hotel from the accommodation where I'd spent the last few nights near the base of the mountain. Sun poured in through the windshield, warming my face despite the crispness in the air. My suitcase was in the back, packed full of dirty hiking clothes and boots for the flight home tomorrow. The weight of those hiking clothes felt different now—not just the physical grime of three days on the mountain, but the emotional residue of all I'd confronted and finally begun to understand. I was bringing home more than I'd carried up.

Three days of mountain climbing with Jonas, and now emptiness. Yet I was not alone. For the first time since that break-up text had devastated my world, I felt completeness inside, as though something long broken had finally begun to mend.

My wealth wasn't what I'd anticipated when I initially arrived in New Zealand. It wasn't getting back the life I'd lost or creating an entirely new one. My wealth was peace—acceptance of who I now was: a different sort of father than I'd intended to be, but still a father. Not as I had been, with bedtime stories every night and outings every weekend, but as I now could be—steadfast, patient, loving from whatever distance my children required. The treasure I'd been seeking wasn't buried on some distant peak, but in the resilient heart I'd carried with me all along.

All the lessons of the last ten years—body, love, tribe, patience, removing addictions to personal growth—had been pointing to this realization. That picture of my younger self had been the initial indication of the truth: rescuing the innocent boy I once was, would rescue the man I had become. I rescued him, and he rescued me in return.

I grinned in the rearview mirror. The man staring back was not the shattered man who'd shown up days before unsure of his role called a father. This man had context and had made peace with his narrative.

My hand had reached involuntarily to the empty chair, as though in search of a warm, soft feminine hand to clasp. Maybe someday. The idea no longer filled me with regret or nervousness but with gentle possibility.

The road took a sharp turn, and before me was the lake that had seen me undergo my transformations. The airport and my Australian life beyond it beckoned—an existence I was now prepared to live, not just survive.

I was born in Melbourne, but I no longer feel a deep connection to it. Even the memories of my childhood, my parents, and my early years feel like they belong to someone else. I've travelled such a long road—from migrating to Western Australia, through the hope and promise of early marriage and parenthood, through the devastation of divorce, the deep love I found with Michaela, the rediscovery of acceptance with my windsurfing tribe, and the loss of identity—until finally arriving here, in this place of peace and acceptance.

Then, with striking clarity, a realisation settled over me: if I had been so deeply affected by the separation, how much more must my children have suffered? They were younger, more vulnerable, their sense of safety anchored in the idea of family unity. While I struggled in the storm of my own grief, they were left to navigate theirs without the life experience or emotional tools—even the ones I lacked.

My most basic failing, in the moments I had strength, was not always making space for their pain. I was consumed—by loss, by confusion, by the overwhelming task of building something new with Michaela while trying to stay afloat. I gave the best of what I had, and I never stopped loving my children. But there were times I could only show up in fragments—imperfectly, inconsistently—not from apathy, but from emotional depletion.

But I've learned something crucial: my ability to empathise didn't vanish—it was buried beneath grief and shame. And now, with clearer eyes and a healing heart, I understand how much more they needed from me. Not perfection. Not a solution. Just presence. Steady, unwavering, honest presence.

That is what I hope to offer now—freely and patiently. With a love that has never dimmed, not even under the weight of time or silence. Children learn more from what we do than from what we say. For years, I was a father hanging by a thread, waging silent battles, trying to make sense of a future I hadn't chosen. There were glimpses of hope—days when the light broke through. But my children didn't need surface optimism or forced cheer. They needed to witness real growth. They needed proof that adversity could be faced with dignity, resilience, and grace.

I tried to give them that. In moments, I succeeded. But maybe not often enough to offset the chaos around us. Not enough to outweigh the influence of the world they were growing up in. But I'm still here. Still loving them. Still choosing to be better—for them and for myself.

As I passed a small orchard, suddenly another memory surfaced — Luke and Olivia, their faces alight with excitement as we drove to a mandarin and orange orchard on Perth's outskirts years ago. I held Olivia's small hand in mine as we wandered between rows of trees, the autumn sun warming our backs. Luke raced ahead, his blonde hair catching the light as he darted between trees, searching for the perfect fruit.

"Not that one, Dad!" Luke called, pointing to a mandarin I'd been about to pick. "It's got a bruise. We need the best ones!"

I smiled, letting my hand drop. Even at 13, his standards were exacting, his focus absolute.

Olivia tugged at my sleeve, pointing up at a particularly ripe orange mandarin just beyond her reach. "That one, Daddy. It's perfect."

I lifted her, her little body light in my arms, so she could pluck it herself. The pride in her eyes as she cradled her selection was worth every kilometre of the drive.

Later, as we sat in the van, juice from fresh-picked fruit running down our chins, I watched my children laughing together and felt a completeness I couldn't articulate. These ordinary moments—picking fruit on a sunny day—would linger in their memories, I hoped, long after they'd forgotten the expensive Christmas gifts or elaborate birthday parties.

I rounded another bend in the road, the lake coming into view again from a different angle. These small adventures were more than just weekend activities. They were investments in connection, bridges across whatever divides might come. In the simple act of doing things together, we formed bonds that sometimes words alone couldn't forge. Another memory flashed before me as I glanced at a mountain bike trail visible from the road.

---•●•---

"Careful on the descent," I called to Luke as he navigated his mountain bike down a particularly steep trail. At 12, his confidence sometimes outpaced his skill resulting in some big crashes, but his determination never wavered.

"I've got it, Dad!" he shouted back, his bike bouncing over rocks and roots with increasing control. The rush of seeing him conquer a challenge he'd been practicing for weeks spread warmth through my chest—a father's pride that transcended any medals or formal achievements.

That evening, as we cleaned mud from our bikes together, Luke looked up at me with those serious blue eyes. "Next time, can we try the black trail?"

"One step at a time," I laughed, ruffling his hair. "Master the blue ones first."

He nodded, already mapping the skills he'd need to advance. That was Luke—always looking ahead, planning his next conquest. Only weeks later he'd ride a black trail with a 20-foot log ride along its wet crest followed by a ten foot drop off back into the trail below. Even then, I recognized the same drive that had pushed me forward throughout my life, for better or worse.

The mountain loomed in my rearview mirror as I continued along the road. I passed a small restaurant with a wood-fired pizza oven visible through the open doors, and suddenly I was back in our kitchen with Olivia.

---•●•---

"Like this, Dad?" she asked, her small hands covered in flour as she tried to roll pasta dough into thin sheets.

"Perfect," I assured her, though the thickness was uneven, and the edges ragged. "You're a natural."

Her face lit up with praise, a smile breaking through the serious concentration she'd been wearing. At nine, with her low muscle tone making fine motor skills challenging, each small victory in the kitchen was hard-won and precious.

"Can I put the sauce on?" she asked eagerly, already reaching for the wooden spoon.

"Absolutely. It's your creation tonight."

As we worked side by side in the warm kitchen, chill music playing softly in the background, I marvelled at her persistence. Where other children might have given up in frustration, Olivia simply tried again, her determination a quiet force that moved mountains in small, steady steps.

Later, as we sat at the dinner table eating our slightly misshaped but delicious pizza, I caught her watching me for approval with each bite I took. The simple joy in her eyes when I declared it "the best pizza in Perth" was a wealth I'd carry through darker days ahead.

I slowed the car as I passed a paddock where several horses grazed peacefully. A young girl was taking a riding lesson, and I was instantly transported to Olivia's early lessons.

———————— •●• ————————

"Dad, you're squeezing!" Olivia giggled as her small hands gripped the reins of her pony. It was her third riding lesson, and her confidence was growing with each session.

"Sorry, sweetheart," I laughed, consciously relaxing my grip on her waist as I walked alongside. My instinct to protect warred with her need for independence— a battle that would play out in countless ways throughout our relationship.

The riding instructor, a patient woman with sun-weathered skin, nodded approvingly. "She's finding her balance. You can step back a bit, Dad."

Taking that step back—literally and figuratively—was harder than I'd expected and never did I think relinquishing custody of her would be the ultimate stepping back. But the pride on Olivia's face as she guided the pony around the ring without my support, was worth every anxious moment.

"I'm doing it!" she called, her voice ringing with triumph. "Dad, look! I'm doing it myself!"

"You sure are," I answered, my heart swelling with a bittersweet mixture of pride and the first faint recognition that my job as her father was not to hold on forever, but to prepare her to ride solo when the time came.

These things had been more than diversions. They'd been lifelines, bridges across the growing chasm between us. In doing things together, we'd found connections that sometimes eluded us in our separate worlds alone. The distractions had provided hope, normalcy, and stability—something constant to hold on to in the storm.

Maybe that was another key to moving forward: not merely speaking of healing but making actual possibilities for it. I did not try to mend all things at once, but I made small moments that had the potential to become something more resilient.

My own fear of the circumstance—the loss, the unknown future—had held me back from offering the level of compassion I now know my children needed, and perhaps even the compassion I needed to extend to myself. I felt the love deeply but often struggled to express it in the way I intended. Communication between us was sometimes strained or disrupted, and those gaps only deepened the emotional distance I was trying so hard to bridge. There was even a time when a phone I'd given Olivia to help us stay in touch was no longer available to her, and the silence that followed was crushing.

I pulled over at a scenic lookout near the airport hotel, needing a moment to gather my thoughts. The landscape before me—rolling green valleys, distant peaks cloaked in soft light—seemed to echo all the paths left unexplored in my life. As I stared out, my thoughts turned to Wayne—the man who had become part of my children's daily lives, while I had gradually shifted into a background role. Over time, my involvement had dwindled to brief dinners or afternoon walks with Olivia, and then, eventually, silence.

Four months earlier, I had made one last effort to reach across the divide. To make peace, not for myself alone, but for the sake of the children we both now had connections to. I wrote a letter—simple, sincere, and offered in goodwill. It read:

"16/9/24

Hi Wayne,

I am contacting you out of goodwill and hope it will be reciprocated. I've recently mentioned to Dianne via email, Luke, and Olivia via text that I believe it's time we met and the reason why I feel this is long overdue after you rejected my initial request some years ago.

The reason I'm offering you the opportunity is that you choose to live with my kids. They are directly and adversely affected by this situation without you and I having a plutonic relationship. It's unhealthy for them to feel unable to share their complete life and challenges with me as their biological father. They certainly don't need any major life events lessened by this inability to share their experiences in the future.

I had also provided Dianne with my phone number via email for you to call me to arrange this as I am also hoping you might be willing to initiate some goodwill. To date you have not called me which is very concerning as you *perhaps don't share my views about the importance of the situation I mention until now.*

I hold the expectation that you respect Luke and Olivia's ability to have their father know and understand who is in their lives as it's my reasonable expectation to be respected for the same purpose.

The implications of the continuing damage by ignoring my requirement to meet you for the purpose above by respecting my kids and myself can't be underestimated. Enough damage has been done and I believe it's time for the reverse. Further status quo is not in the best interests of all concerned.

At this point I will leave it for you to reach out to me before too long to arrange a coffee or something else to meet you.

I have sent this note to Luke, Olivia and Dianne updating them with my intention and concerns. I think it's important they understand this process and implications of your living relationship with them and my intent to have an understanding of whom they live with. Looking forward to your contact Wayne and of course if you'd like Dianne with you. Feel free.

Regards,

Mark Woodley"

I wanted both Wayne and Dianne to understand my need to meet Wayne without any confusion, so I wrote to Dianne directly and posted her letter the same time as Wayne's.

"16/9/24

Hi Dianne,

I've provided you a letter of which has been sent to Wayne recently. It's worth reading to get an understanding of why.

I hope that you support my need to meet Wayne as Luke and Olivia's biological farther.

I've requested to meet Wayne yrs ago without the respect of acknowledgement of my wish and concern for the situation.

I hope Wayne has the courage and decency to oblige my request out of goodwill and you support this too respecting Luke, Olivia's, and my situation. Ultimately, it's whether Wayne respects me, Luke and Olivia or doesn't. And not doing so is damming towards the three of us. We have paid an enormous price for this difficult situation, and I hope it gets resolved.

Anyway, out of respect to you, I am informing you of my actions and hopes. Luke and Olivia have the same letter to Wayne so they things are in the open.

Mark"

I remember how my fingers trembled—an uneasy mix of anger, hope, and vulnerability—as I slid the letters into their envelopes. Every word had been weighed carefully, written not just for my own peace of mind, but for the emotional wellbeing of my children. I was trying to build a bridge—to show that even through pain, adults could set aside resentment and pride for the greater good. I wanted Luke and Olivia to see that maturity could prevail, and that their lives didn't need to be divided by unspoken tensions.

The response? Silence from both Wayne and Dianne. A quiet that spoke volumes—heavy and difficult to bear.

It was the first time I had reached out to Wayne in years. Prior to that, I had sent several messages through Olivia's phone, not out of spite, but in the hope it would reach him directly. I was frustrated, yes—but I still wrote with care and intention. Extending an olive branch. Hoping that future interactions—birthdays, milestones, everyday transitions—might be made easier if there was at least a baseline of mutual respect and understanding. I wrote…

"4/12/2019

Hello Wayne, Mark Woodley here, Olivia and Luke's dad. It's time to meet the father of the kids you live with. You have been living and caring for kids, especially my little daughter Olivia, for some time now. The awkwardness of the current situation for the kids is not right and unfair for them. A letter was sent to you a year ago offering to meet, but I understand it was intercepted. It indicated the importance of the meeting. I'm not sure if you received it in the end, but it suggested a coffee at Elixir Cafe. It would be very difficult for all if anything happened by accident with the kids whilst in your care and not knowing me and contacting me.

Anyway, the offer has been made directly to you now. How about a morning next week? This has nothing to do with Dianne. Let me know.

Mark Woodley"

I tried over the years, and I'll keep trying—to show my children their father's love and care. Maybe that's what matters most: not getting everything right but never giving up. That I kept knocking, even when the door stayed closed.

I turned the ignition and eased back onto the road. As the car moved forward, so did my memory—to the time when Michaela left, and I hit rock bottom. The physical challenges I threw myself into, like the windsurfing marathon on Christmas Day, weren't just ways to pass the time. They were acts of survival. My way of telling the world—and myself—that I wasn't going to be undone by grief.

As Jonas challenged my thinking on those long mountain hikes, the more I began to confront the full weight of the past. And with it came the regret—regret for the years lost with my kids. Years when I was absent or when they chose distance that I didn't fully understand. I wasn't invited to Luke's 18th or 21st birthdays. There was nearly a year without contact. At the time, I searched for reasons, for something that would help make sense of it.

Now, I see more clearly: the reasons don't matter as much as his feelings. Whatever shaped his decisions, they were valid to him—and that's what counts. My role as a father is to honour that, not fight against it. To keep showing up with love, patience, and humility—no matter how long it takes.

I missed Luke's graduation, a milestone that was especially difficult to be absent from. I remembered how important school admissions had once been in our family—planning for New Zealand, securing spots in Melbourne, even buying a house there. In the end, it was a late acceptance in Perth that defined the course.

On the day of his graduation, I sat in my car outside the venue. I wanted so badly to go in. But I didn't. My emotions were raw. The weight of everything felt too heavy. I was afraid—afraid of who I might see, how I might react, and what it might do to him. So, I stayed in the car. Luke marked that milestone without me, and that pain still lives with me.

There were other moments, too—like Olivia's 16th birthday. A milestone for any young woman. I wasn't there that day either. Though I tried to reach out, it wasn't the same as being present. That absence cut deep. I imagine it hurt her too, whether or not she said it aloud.

Over time, I felt myself slipping from my children's lives—not by choice, but by a slow erosion of connection, shaped by hurt, silence, and circumstances I and they couldn't always control. Their emotional needs were caught in the crosscurrents of two households, and despite everyone's best efforts, it often felt like no one was winning.

I don't believe anyone meant to make things harder for them. I genuinely believe that each person around them was trying to make the best choices they could at the time. But someday, I hope there's room for an honest conversation—for Luke and Olivia to speak freely about what they experienced, and for everyone to listen. No defences. Just openness, humility, and care. Because that's what all children deserve.

And from me, my son deserves a sincere apology. Not to relieve my guilt, but because he matters. His feelings matter. And I didn't always honour that. I failed him during crucial moments—not from a lack of love, but from my own internal battles I was trying to survive. I lost sight of what he needed because I was overwhelmed. And while I had my reasons, I now know that outcomes matter more than intentions.

What Luke lived through, what he felt, what was missing—these are the facts. They deserve to be acknowledged with honesty, not explained away. Because only by facing those truths can healing begin—for all of us.

On August 20th, 2022, I dropped Olivia off at her mums to stay for good. It was one of the hardest days of my life—sacrificing my final shared custody time with my dear daughter into a household with a stranger unwilling to meet me. But strangely, in the time since, I've found a quiet kind of peace within the unfolding narrative of my life. People enter your world, and sometimes they leave it again. The agonizing pain I endured when my children were removed from my daily life far too soon was not something to "get over." It became something I had to learn how to live with, to survive—not to erase, but to carry with grace.

The road sloped gently downward toward the airport hotel, its schist-stone appearance growing clearer. My flight wasn't until tomorrow, but something within me stirred—a quiet urging to return to the mountain once more. Not to climb it again today, but to honour what it had given me. I made a silent promise to myself: I would return to its base one day—not as the man who had ascended in pain, but as the man who had emerged with peace.

This mountain had become my teacher. It trained me to anticipate difficulty, to trust in preparation, and to walk with compassion—for others and for myself. Where once I had looked upon it with regret for the life that never came to be, I now saw it as a source of strength, of love, and of hope. No longer a monument to what I had lost, but a beacon for what still could be.

When confronted with the most difficult sections of the ascent, I had learned to master the art of believing in the unseen—of forging a path forward even when none was visible. Recovery from addiction had been no different. I had pushed my body to its physical limits in order to reach the wounds buried deep within, to expose them to air and light so they could finally begin to heal.

I remembered gripping a wire rope as I climbed that smooth near vertical ridge, sheer drops yawning on either side. I had breathed with precision—slow, intentional, steady—the same breathwork I had relied on when resisting the pull toward numbness through alcohol. Both the mountain's steep face and the bottle offered the same outcome if misjudged: a fall into darkness. But with presence, courage, and care, I had chosen to keep climbing.

I pulled into the airport hotel parking lot—the journey from the mountain complete, but the larger journey just beginning. My mind drifted back to the rugged slope where I had once hiked, deliberately leaning into discomfort as turbulent memories surfaced in conversations with Jonas. It was there I'd come to understand: growth lives on the other side of suffering. And beyond that growth, there isn't more pain—but rather, the freedom to love without walls.

Up on the mountain, I had felt an unfamiliar emptiness—not one born of loss, but of readiness. It was a quiet void, newly carved, not to echo but to hold. A space for new connections, new meanings. My heart, no longer weighed down, now had room to expand. I wasn't seeking comfort anymore—I had something to offer. I was ready for conversations shaped by the light of tomorrow, not the shadows of yesterday.

The butterflies and crickets had been scattered on the rocks around me that day, and I thought of Elli. She had been my butterfly—my good luck charm, my quiet symbol of beauty and hope. Their presence felt like a sign, whispering truths I hadn't yet permitted myself to believe. It was as if Elli herself had joined me there, guiding me into a space safe enough to heal, brave enough to grow.

I remembered that one misstep on the narrow ridge—the jolt of panic, the sharp inhale, the desperate reach for a handhold that kept me from sliding to my death. That moment crystalized a truth I'd overlooked for too long: I had to live. Not just survive—but truly live. To savour what was still possible. To tread carefully forward, knowing that one wrong step—whether in love or in family—could alter everything.

I sat in the parked vehicle for a long moment before switching off the engine. I'd always loved being a father—that much had never changed. What had changed was my understanding: I wasn't built to parent alone, any more than my children were built to be passed between homes, carrying emotional luggage neither had packed. We had all been navigating a reality chosen by someone else, each of us doing what we could to survive.

Tomorrow, I would return home. But I would carry something back with me—not just memories of alpine winds and narrow trails, but a heart that had been changed. The journey wasn't over. In many ways, it had only just begun. There would be hard days still—moments of disappointment, moments of connection. Failures. Joy. All of it. But this time, I would meet them with open hands, not clenched fists. I was ready now.

My wealth had always been with me, buried beneath the rubble of grief, pride, and fear. It wasn't the picture-perfect family I once chased, nor the redemption story I tried to force. It was something softer: acceptance. Peace. Not in perfection—but in presence. It lived here, in the mountains of the New Zealand Southern Alps, where my heart felt at home. And with that clarity came something else: the quiet confidence that I could still be the father my children needed. Even if it looked nothing like I once imagined.

The next morning at the airport checking in my bags, I turned around to face the sunlit mountain though the large floor to ceiling windows, lifting my eyes for one final look at the peak. For years, I'd lived suspended between the anger of what I had lost and the fear of what might never be. But now, standing once more beneath her towering shadow, I felt neither.

What stirred within me instead was a quiet certainty.

Whatever lay ahead, I would face it—no longer burdened by expectation or crushed by regret. The mountain had shown me that the climb was never really about the summit. It was about the transformation that unfolded with every step. She had offered me strength, clarity, and the inspiration to begin again—to write a new chapter built on meaning, presence, and the slow, patient rebuilding of love with my beautiful children.

She had never asked to be conquered. She had only waited—for me to arrive ready to listen, to understand, to heal. This place had become sacred ground. A landscape in which I could interpret the past, process old wounds, and finally see meaning in the moments that had once brought me to my knees.

I knew now that New Zealand would remain part of my life—not just as a personal refuge, but as a future place of connection. One day, I would bring Luke and Olivia here as young adults. Let them explore the trails, feel the wind, see the peaks—and find their own clarity in the wild beauty that had given me mine.

My dream, once pushed aside, still lived. It wasn't too late.

"Thank you," I whispered—to the mountain, to Jonas, my own heart, which had at last found its way home.

13

FROM THE SUMMIT

Reflections for the father still climbing

I stared out of the plane's small window, my eyes locked on the snow-capped peaks slipping past beneath us as we headed westward toward Melbourne then Perth. In the distance, I saw her—the mountain. The sharp peak that had held me captive over the past few days now stood out proudly against the rugged landscape, etched into memory. It was there that Jonas had spoken. There that my healing had taken root.

I pictured myself on her slopes again, climbing steadily through silence, deep in trance, speaking to Jonas as though he were beside me. That mountain had become my confessional—each step unlocking a memory, a truth, a reconciliation I had buried long ago. It was where my past was finally digested, piece by piece, in the raw honesty that only solitude could allow.

To an onlooker, I must have seemed impossibly alone—a tiny figure navigating the sheer face of a massive range, dwarfed by granite cliffs and sharp, jutting bluffs. I saw only three cars over those few days at the mountain and saw no one. But I was never truly alone.

I was in the most powerful company of all: my own truth. The mountain. And Jonas—his voice ever-present, thought-provoking, unwavering. Together, they witnessed every ascent. Every step of my return to myself.

The soft vibration and steady hum of the engines lulled me into deep reflection as I kept my eyes fixed on her—*that* sharp, distinguished peak—growing smaller with each passing moment. Slowly, she faded into the sprawling silhouette of the Southern Alps, dissolving into the trailing horizon like a memory slipping out of reach. As she vanished, a familiar dream-like stillness settled over me—the same surreal calm I'd felt the moment Jonas disappeared. It was as if both the mountain and Jonas had retreated together, their work done, leaving me changed.

My mind drifted to when many years ago I received a Father's Day card from Luke. His handprint, tenderly saved from his first school years, was a bittersweet memory from the past. His tiny hand, written in blue pen with the date, "1-9-06" scrawled beside it, was a time when our bond was physical and literal—his hand in mine as we walked streets, as we constructed Lego towers together so tall that I'd hold him up so he could place each piece higher and higher, as I taught him to skid 180s on his first BMX bike. This plain white paper outline, now so diminutive compared to the young man's hand in which it was once contained, reminds me that although physical ties may diminish over time and circumstances, the impression children make upon a father's heart never decreases, regardless of distance.

I reflected on the journey that had brought me to this moment—37,000 feet above the earth, heading west toward Perth. Behind me lay valleys of darkness, broken terrain, and mountain trails so steep I once thought I'd never make it through. A single text message had shattered my life a decade ago. In seconds, everything I had built—the family I cherished, the business I shaped with grit and persistence, the identity of a devoted father—was split apart, scattered into pieces I struggled for years to gather again. Some were never recovered.

This wasn't a victory lap. Not even close. As I stared out into the deep blue skyline, where the atmosphere began to darken into the edges of space, I felt awe—but not triumph. I reached for my notepad, the one I had used during the hikes, where thoughts first began to untangle in the clean mountain air. An urge stirred in me again—to keep writing, to continue shaping the insights and reconciliations that had emerged beside Jonas, in that sacred stillness the mountain offered.

This journey I've recorded isn't a tale of heroism. It's a trail map drawn by a father who stumbled countless times, who crawled more than he walked, and who at times lost sight of the summit. I haven't written these pages to assign blame or to ask for sympathy. I wrote them because, ten years ago, I needed someone—anyone—to show me it was possible to survive. That the weight wouldn't crush me forever. That peace could be found—one day.

I learned slowly. Not through neat breakthroughs—but through mostly unwittingly, raw, messy reactions to life's harshest lessons. So many moments were unclear, even senseless. I wandered in grief, made mistakes, carried shame. For a long time, I relied only on hindsight to make sense of it all. But more recently, I've been guided by something else—by the quiet, steady voice that surfaced beside Jonas. The one that had been there all along. My own heart finally heard.

Each step, each misstep, each pause in the darkness was part of a larger unfolding. I see that now. And if there's any purpose to these reflections, it's to serve as a map for someone else in the dark. To say: *you are not alone, and you can survive this too.*

My divorce was nothing special. The circumstances might vary from one story to the next, but the pain—that's always the same. The trauma of knowing your children will grow up in separate homes, possibly guided by adult strangers. The suffocating fear that your role as a father might slowly fade as they adapt to a life without your daily presence. The crushing financial pressure as everything you've built is split in two. The expectation to keep providing, even as you're quietly rejected. And the question that lingers on quiet nights: *Will they remember who I was to them when we were still a whole family?*

My head tilted slightly forward as the descent began toward the first stopover—Melbourne. I glanced out the window, where cotton-ball clouds floated above the sprawling cityscape below. It was a world I'd once known well, decades ago. The curve of the bay was unmistakable, and the rise of Arthur's Seat stood clear above the tightly packed suburbs. I remembered when those hills were bordered by open paddocks, the ones I'd drive past after long days selling Yellow Pages advertising. Still full of energy, returning home to renovate our house into the early evening—newly married, fuelled by hope and ambition.

Our wedding reception had been held atop Arthur's Seat—just fifty people, a modest celebration shadowed by urgency. Dianne's father had fallen ill, and the date was brought forward to ensure he could be there. Even then, beneath the warm glow of wedding speeches and clinking glasses, I knew we weren't ready. The day was layered with unspoken fears and compromised optimism. Youthful hope all converged into a choice that neither of us fully understood at the time.

Perhaps, with more time, our hearts might have spoken differently. It wasn't just Dianne and me who paid the price for a commitment made without due consideration—but also Luke and Olivia. As parents, we share the responsibility for how our incompatibility impacted our kids.

My gaze followed down to Mentone Beach—my birthplace of another world. It was here that wind and water first became my sanctuary, offering peace through adolescence in Melbourne, and later in adulthood along the coast of Albany and Mandurah, Western Australia.

Memories flooded back—teenage summers embraced by the sea breeze, wild winter storms that shaped my resilience, and friendships formed on the sand and water. Most of those friends were eventually lost, some claimed by drugs or the chaos that follows. One in particular—Martin—my closest high school mate, would never see adulthood. His death etched a scar I carried silently of the vulnerability of addictions.

I remembered meeting other windsurfers, older than me—Litz and Chris, two towering German brothers. They introduced me to a place I'd never been: Perth. Their photos showed windswept, crystal blue waters, whitecaps dancing in endless sunshine. After Dad passed, and my small business back home began to unravel, those images felt like more than just inspiration—they were a calling.

At twenty-two, I sold up, hitched a trailer to my car, and placed Sabre, my Kelpie, in the passenger seat. With a little over two thousand dollars in savings and not a single contact in Perth, I drove the three thousand kilometres west. It took three days. But I felt it deeply—this was where the wind and water could breathe new life into me. It was my instinct to start again. To leave behind the weight of loss—Dad's early death, my turbulent relationship with Mum, and the heartbreak with Sarah, my first love.

Sarah reminded me so much of Michaela—graceful, traditional, a natural beauty. An old-school soul in a modern world. Rare and valuable, as I would come to learn.

Reflecting on that bold move across the continent reminded me of the feeling I'd had in New Zealand these past few days. It was familiar. Just as Western Australia once waited patiently to welcome me into a new chapter, so too, now, does New Zealand—quietly holding space for something meaningful to begin again.

I kept staring. The sky was clear between the thick clouds. From my window seat during descent, I spotted Ricketts Point Beach and could make out the faint but familiar bike path I'd followed so often in my secondary school years, winding from home in Beaumaris to the school grounds. My mind flooded with memories—hauling my

197

windsurfer strapped awkwardly to my ten-speed bike, racing to the beach after school or early on windy weekend mornings. I could just make out the cliff near the jetty where I used to launch, swimming the board out past the pier catch the windline.

That cliff held more than just adrenaline. It was where I spent countless evenings with a beer in hand, alone, breaking down in the aftermath of Mum and Dad's separation. A lonely lookout where alcohol became a quiet teacher in the art of numbing pain. I remembered, too, the morning I rode to school in a winter blizzard, my clothes soaked in rain and face wet with tears—Mum had been evicted the night before.

Further along the coastline, I could see the outline of my old primary school. That's where I first felt the tender pulse of affection—my first crush in Year three. Her name was Natasha, a blonde Russian girl who stayed etched in my memory.

I craned my neck, reluctant to lose sight of the suburbs that shaped me. But the plane veered, and my view shifted to the freeway running toward Geelong and down to Ocean Grove—where many of my weekends and school holidays were spent with my beloved grandparents. The place I had made the timber tower so many years ago. I remembered those simple, grounding moments in their home—their warmth and wisdom still close to my heart. Years later, I stood proudly as a family man delivering the eulogy at each of their funerals.

One of my most treasured gifts to myself came on my fortieth birthday, when I brought Luke, Olivia, and my ex-wife back to Melbourne. I just wanted my kids to meet their great-grandfather—to walk with them into his workshop where the scent of timber and oil lingered like it had for decades. To see the same yard where I had found that photograph of my young self after completing the timber tower project—34 years earlier.

All of it—the bike rides, the heartbreak, the crushes, the evictions, the ocean breeze, the sound of tools in my grandfather's shed—hit me at once, vivid as ever. The tears came without warning, soft but certain, as the plane sliced gently through the grey, descending cloud cover that marked our arrival into Melbourne.

Then a jolt—turbulence. The seat gave a subtle shuffle beneath me. I smiled faintly, recognising it instantly. That big Melbourne westerly was blowing strong. I could read the clouds like an old friend—those same cloud lines I had watched hundreds of times while windsurfing.

And just like that, another wave of thought surged through me.

Luke was born in Melbourne. I remember the day like it was yesterday—along with the day Olivia was born, they remain the proudest moments of my life. I had cut his umbilical cord, severing him into the world, welcoming him into life as his own being. That singular act of fatherhood—so intimate, so symbolic— stayed etched in my memory.

As the plane taxied to the terminal, I breathed deeply—just as I had on the mountain when I thought I could go no further. That same discipline, that same grounding. The injustice I felt was acute. Moments ago, flying directly above the very place where Luke and I had once shared a beautiful closeness, now fractured by time, circumstance, and choices beyond my control.

And then I thought of Olivia. I had also cut her umbilical cord, a moment just as sacred. Yet years later, I had found myself making another painful severance— letting go of custody to provide her stability, even at great personal cost. How ironic, I mused, that once again I was preparing to cut a cord—this time, not of a child, but of a chapter. A chapter still deeply influenced by the past and by my former wife.

As the cabin door opened at the terminal, I glanced across the aisle and noticed a man around my age. For a moment, I wondered—was he, too, a father navigating the silent grief of distance? Had he also faced the quiet ache of seeing his children grow up at arm's length?

I knew I wasn't the only one. And somehow, that knowledge brought a strange comfort. A shared fraternity of separated fathers—wounded, resilient, still standing.

There's a quiet truth that weighs heavily on many separated fathers—a truth rarely voiced and with no real avenue for redress: the deep pain of being deliberately excluded from your children's lives, while a stranger—someone who has made no effort to establish a respectful connection—takes up space in the kids home. It feels unnatural, even violating, to watch from a distance as your role is overwritten without consent or conversation.

This isn't about pride or entitlement. It's about what such silence communicates—not just to me, but to my children. It sends a message that their biological father doesn't matter. That he is somehow peripheral. That the relationship between them and me is not important enough to warrant the simple courtesy of mutual respect and acknowledgment. That message, however unintentional, can cut deeply.

Being gradually distanced from the family I helped build—especially during the critical years of my children's development—has felt less like a singular loss and more like an ongoing grief. A grief that is hard to name but impossible to ignore. During a period of profound personal difficulty, another adult began playing a significant role in my children's lives. There was no effort to foster unity or understanding for the benefit of the kids.

I wasn't kept in the loop on important details about Olivia's wellbeing, nor included in shared memories like birthday celebrations, Christmases, or milestones. Whether intentional or not, the result was the same: I felt like a ghost in my own children's lives. A co-parent in name, but not in practice. Expected to support from a distance yet rarely acknowledged.

I share this not to cast blame, but to voice an experience I know is shared by many fathers: the ache of invisibility, the hope for inclusion, and the belief that respectful communication is always in the best interest of the children.

Regarding the new adult figure in my children's lives, I can only hope that, over time, my children will be able to discern for themselves what consistency, openness, and emotional presence look like. Not in contrast to anyone else, but through reflection on their own lived experiences. My wish is that, despite my imperfections, they'll come to understand the quiet power of showing up—even in hardship. That love can be resilient, patient, and enduring, even when it isn't loud or always visible.

When the message of separation arrived, it brought with it more than heartbreak. I felt a profound concern—not only for myself, but for the long-term emotional wellbeing of our children. I sensed then that the road ahead would be complicated, filled with challenges in communication and coordination. During the relationship, I had noticed a pattern of decisions being made independently, and I worried this might continue post-separation.

My concern wasn't rooted in control or criticism—it came from a deep belief that children benefit most when both parents remain active, informed, and collaborative in their upbringing. I held onto that belief even as our family dynamic shifted. I wanted to remain a steady presence—not just in a few moments of joy, but through the difficult ones as well. Because co-parenting, when done well, isn't about agreement on everything. It's about equal and shared commitment to the children's best interests, even when the path is hard to walk.

Soon after take-off to Perth, I loosened the seatbelt and shifted in my seat, giving myself room—physically and emotionally—as the weight of reflection continued to surface with every stroke of the pen. Outside, the sky deepened into a rich navy, streaked with fading salmon light across the western horizon. As dusk settled in, I knew I had to confront the last few obstacles to healing before arriving home.

My thoughts began to slow, returning to a question that had lingered quietly throughout the journey: Had I been too harsh in my self-examination these past few days? I welcomed judgment—especially from those who mattered most.

Perhaps, in some ways, I had gone too far. I'd called myself an alcoholic, which might not fit everyone's definition, but for me, it was honest. I'd rather dive into the deep end and be seen swimming than linger at the edge claiming I got wet.

This was never about seeking sympathy. It was about truth. About clarity. About ensuring the record was set straight—not just for others, but especially for my children. They deserved to understand. Not to excuse, not even necessarily to forgive—but to know. To make sense of the past, and in doing so, better navigate their own lives with awareness, empathy, and strength.

More than anything, they deserved to know this: My love for them never faltered. It was constant. Unyielding. Absolute.

I came into this world flawed, as we all do. One of my vulnerabilities was a sensitivity to anxiety, and a tendency to suppress it. For me, that suppression took the form of alcohol. It wasn't a deliberate decision, at least not in the beginning. It was the instinct of an unprepared mind trying to manage unresolved pain the only way it knew how.

In adulthood, my reliance on alcohol was fuelled by a mix of pride, inexperience, and a lack of self-confidence. I didn't know how to ask for help. Or maybe I did, but I lacked the courage to reach for it. That help eventually came—too late for some moments I wish I could go back and change—but thankfully, not too late to grow. After the separation, professional support became the only viable path forward, and I followed it with intention and humility.

I was also born with strengths. One of them is the refusal to give up. To keep going, no matter how bruised or lost. And even though I came close to the edge more than once, I made a quiet vow: that my story would be told. That the truth would be known. That those who shaped it—me included—would be seen not through blame, but with honesty. Most of all, I hoped my children would one day come to know me fully—not just the mistakes or the moments of absence, but the love that never wavered underneath it all.

Understanding takes time. Messages of love from both Luke and Oliva during my time away had brought a real hope—a sign that love had survived the distance. That perhaps it was only now beginning to take its truest shape: one forged through truth, hardship, and time.

There's a certain peace that comes with taking responsibility. It doesn't erase the past, but it offers steadier sleep. Sitting here on this plane, with nothing to distract me, I find myself thinking again about how painful it is when a parent-child bond is slowly eroded—not by absence, but by tension, influence, and circumstance.

I wasn't the only one affected. My daughter felt it too, in ways she may not yet be able to name. Luke carried it as well. I sensed it in their silences, in the hesitancy of their words after long absences. We were all impacted by a dynamic none of us chose—one that caused confusion and pain in its wake. But I still believe that healing is possible—for all of us.

Over time, I noticed a gradual shift. When a new figure entered their lives, things changed. Whether intentional or not, communication between their mother and me became more limited, and over time, more distant. I often felt shut out of the day-to-day details of my children's lives, without clarity on how or why that shift occurred.

I don't speak from resentment. I speak from concern—from a father's heart, still aching to understand. I wasn't questioning the presence of someone new, but I did begin to question why my presence felt increasingly diminished. Why had my role—built on years of care and closeness—been allowed to fade?

It's not all about biology. It's about what children internalize when one parent quietly disappears from daily life—not by choice, but by circumstances beyond their control. What does it teach them about love? About loyalty? About family?

These are the questions I carry. Not in anger. But with a deep, enduring hope: that I might still be part of their story—not in the background, not as a holiday guest, but as their father.

This isn't about one person. It reflects a broader pattern that unfolded after the separation—decisions made without collaboration or consultation. I don't know what those choices were rooted in. Fear, maybe. Pain. A desire for simplicity. But whatever the reason, the result was the same: it became harder for me to stay connected to my children in the way I once had.

I imagine it became hard for them too—trying to navigate occasions like birthdays, graduations, and school milestones, always weighing whose comfort mattered more, never sure how to include both parents without upsetting someone. No child should feel that pressure. They should be able to move freely between both their worlds, loved equally, without having to choose sides or suppress parts of their experience.

I've long taken responsibility for my own failings. I've owned the mistakes I made and the times I wasn't the father I wanted to be. I don't expect perfection from others—only reflection. Not for my sake, but for Luke and Olivia's. Because they're the ones who lived between two stories, who often stayed silent about what they lost and what they still longed for.

They deserve more than divided narratives, protected egos and quiet discomfort. They deserve adults who can acknowledge the past, step up with empathy, and work together—however imperfectly—for their future.

As I stared into the soft dark outside the window, my pen slowed. The sharp edge of the emotion I'd been carrying dulled. I took a long breath. And for the first time in a long while, I understood why: acceptance.

The hiking, the writing—it had all helped me digest the past. Not erase it, but to accept it, to find peace and understand it in a new light. This wasn't a surrender.

It was fists down, heart open. And it didn't diminish my love or care for my children. It just meant fatherhood would take a different shape now.

In those first shattered days after Dianne's text message, I didn't know what to do. I ended up sleeping at my business for a few nights, stunned and hollow. My instincts screamed to rage, to blame, to lash out—but I knew any such reaction would only accelerate my collapse. Instead, I turned to professional counselling. That single decision became the seed from which all the later lessons would grow.

There were many lessons—each one vital to my survival, and they didn't come one at a time. They arrived scattered in time like the pieces of my life had become. All loud, and urgent.

Financial stability was slow coming. My frantic attempts to recoup losses through reckless share trading only deepened the wounds. I had to learn discipline in the face of desperation. Learning to make rational decisions—even when consumed by emotion—became a lifeline. Finding purpose in providing for my children and giving my young self the life he deserved gave me a reason to stand each day when nothing else would.

Physical strength became my anchor. When my heart was shattered, when my mind couldn't form a single clear thought, my body became the only place I had control. Windsurfing. Mountain biking with Luke. Every session, every trail, reminded me of what clarity felt like. Alcohol, gambling—all forms of escapism—were nothing but dead weight. Progress needed movement. Reconstruction needed discipline.

Social isolation nearly destroyed me. But then came Cody—met through windsurfing—and others who shared the same passions. Men with their own stories, scars, and resilience. Their company was my scaffolding. I learned that no man rebuilds alone. Brotherhood saved me in a way therapy couldn't. Fellowship isn't a luxury—it's survival.

Meeting Michaela taught me one of the most beautiful and unexpected truths: a broken heart doesn't heal through protection—it heals through love. It's not walls or withdrawal that bring peace, but the courage to remain open. To risk being emotionally wounded again, even when already shattered, was the very path that allowed healing to begin.

Letting go of Isabella, despite the love I had begun to feel for her, was a necessary act of self-preservation. I had to choose my future over my past. I could not walk back into the shadow of alcohol—not even for the hope of love. So, I chose something healthier. I chose the kind of love that doesn't threaten my recovery. I chose self-love with a future built on clarity, not chaos. I chose to prioritise and remain in control of myself.

Patience was tested every day. My texts to Olivia and Luke often went unanswered, met with silence that echoed louder than any words. Their lives moved on without my daily presence—not out of malice, but as their way of navigating a divided world. I came to understand that love doesn't demand instant affirmation. True love shows up, again and again, without expectation. Every unreturned message was not a rejection, but a reflection of their internal conflict—torn between loyalty, safety, and the emotional weight of divided homes.

After losing almost everything, personal growth became my anchor. Rewiring my thoughts through relentless learning, confronting physical limits—like during that Christmas windsurfing marathon—redefined how I processed pain and opened new visions of what healing could look like.

In my darkest moments—lying frozen outside a respite hospital and then contemplating another final exit weeks later—I discovered that even in absolute darkness, a single point of light remained. For me, that light was the six-year-old boy in the photo, the boy with hope in his eyes and dreams yet untouched. His voice, clear and urgent—Don't die, Dad—pulled me back from the edge.

Healing, I've come to learn, isn't about justice or revenge. It's about understanding. It's about choosing to control the only things we ever truly can—our thoughts, our actions, and how we show up for the people we love.

On the 2nd of February 2024, not long after being saved by that moment of white light, I wrote a note to myself on my phone—a small anchor of clarity for challenging times. It now lives beside the photo of young Mark from a decade earlier, a daily reminder of my promise.

My Why:

To use every talent, I've been given. To live in a way that makes me feel I've done justice to myself. I picture my older self one day, sitting on a rocking chair, being asked about his life. I see him nodding with calm conviction, saying:

"Yes, I did that. Yes, I tried that. I gave everything I had. I did everything I could."

That's what I call *young Mark justice.*

Goals

1. To work for freedom
2. Motivated to love and connect with people.
3. To enjoy health, my body and mind.

Done by

1. Building strong business.
2. Living a healthy life
3. Acting with passion
4. Loving connections: Olivia and Luke, friends, and lovers

That's my ideal self.

The more I reflect on the events and people surrounding the circumstances of my fatherhood, the more I see where I've fallen short—especially over the last ten years. And yet, on the other side of that ledger, I also see a wonderful man. A loving father who is loyal, hard-working, intelligent, physically capable, and deeply empathetic. I hope, with time, my children will see the fuller picture too, and that the positive weighs more than the pain.

If there is one lesson that rises above all others in this journey, it's empathy. Empathy for others, and perhaps just as importantly, empathy for myself. I've come to believe this is the antidote to many of life's pains, missteps, and confusions.

Empathy is especially vital when facing the primal urges that arise as a father—urges to protect your children when you're no longer in the home, and when new adults become daily influences in their lives. We live in an advanced, modern society in so many ways, and yet we lack meaningful structures to support the emotional realities of separated families. There's a deep need for systems that honour the ongoing role of each parent, especially when children are adjusting to new relationships in their household. The opportunity for mutual respect among adults—especially between a biological parent and a new partner—could provide immense healing and security for the children involved.

In my case, I often felt like a bystander in my own children's lives. There were attempts to build bridges, but silence met many of them. That silence has left lasting emotional gaps, not just for me, but I believe, for my children too. At times, I felt the decisions being made didn't fully acknowledge the value of my continuing presence as their father.

I recognise now that my own rigid expectations—of continuing to parent as I had before separation—may have been unrealistic. I wanted to continue guiding Luke, sharing life lessons, being his constant. But the reality was more complex, and he made choices that helped him cope with the situation he found himself in. Choices that, while painful for me, are understandable.

My frustration often stemmed from not knowing who was influencing my children in a home I no longer shared. For any parent, there's a deep discomfort in being excluded from understanding the people shaping your child's daily life. Not out of jealousy or control, but from a place of care, responsibility, and an instinctive desire to protect and support. When those bridges aren't built, the absence of connection—intentional or not—can lead to unnecessary tension and unease.

This isn't about assigning blame. It's about acknowledging how complex these transitions can be. I believe this is something worth considering more broadly: how can we, as a society, do better to ensure that children feel secure and that both parents feel respected in post-separation life? How do we create processes that encourage transparency and cooperation rather than silence and division?

Looking back, I believe fear may have shaped many of the dynamics I encountered. Fear of confrontation. Fear of reopening wounds. Fear of unsettling a new, carefully balanced structure. And while I can't speak to the motivations of others, I've chosen not to dwell on what I can't change. My attention remains focused on what I can influence: the wellbeing of my children, and the ongoing effort to repair and nurture our relationship, however imperfectly.

As for legal or moral responsibility, those are questions for a different conversation, one I'm not seeking to resolve here. What I do believe is that this experience has revealed an unmet need—for more thoughtful, emotionally intelligent frameworks that guide families through the challenges of shared parenting, blended households, and evolving relationships.

Because even when family structures change, the bond between parent and child should never be made conditional. That connection deserves to be preserved, honoured, and supported—by all involved.

The mountain gave me perspective. It taught me that peace doesn't come from controlling what was or what might be—but in accepting what is. It taught me to cherish the moments I *do* have with my children, however infrequent or imperfect. I'm grateful I took so many photos over the years—images that capture our love, our connection, and our time together. They are reminders that my bond with Luke and Olivia endures.

New Zealand didn't become the family haven I once imagined, but it became something equally important—a place of profound healing. A perch to gain perspective. And from this view, I can see clearly now: I am still their father. Always have been. Always will be.

To separate dads reading these words, I share these hard-learned lessons:

- Seek professional help immediately—pride will only deepen your suffering.
- Remember your kids absorb everything—your energy sets the tone for their crisis response.
- Protect your financial stability—avoid desperate risks; build your future with discipline.
- Strengthen your body—it's the only vessel strong enough to carry a broken heart and fogged mind.
- Let go of the dependencies—they numb the pain but stall your growth.
- Find your tribe—people who share your passions, and dads who truly understand your struggle.
- Keep reaching out—text, call, show up… even if you're met with silence.
- Don't shut your heart off from love—real healing often begins with emotional risk.
- Commit to self-development—transform pain into growth through conscious effort.
- Face reality head-on—comfortable illusions only delay your recovery.
- Search for the white light of hope—however faint. For me, it was the voice of my younger self in an old photo, the boy I once was, reminding me of the life I promised him.
- Know that healing is not about justice—it's about acceptance, humility, and letting go.

- Turn toward the future—don't let the past define what's still possible.
- Never forget your younger self—he's still inside you, watching. Make him proud.

These lessons won't erase your pain. They won't restore what's been lost.

But perhaps these words will help you find your way through the wilderness that lies between devastation, acceptance and peace. If the slow, hard-won lessons of my own journey can be useful to you—if they help you move forward with even a little more clarity or compassion—then maybe that is something worthwhile.

Some will say I'm just seeking empathy. Others may brush this off entirely with a familiar refrain: "Get over it. Move on. That was years ago." And to those voices, I say—yes, moving on is an option. But it's also the path that often leads to quiet bitterness and resentment. Those are not just emotional burdens—they can become illnesses of the body, the mind, and the spirit.

Time doesn't heal all wounds. Time conceals them—until something unexpected rips them open again: a memory, a silence, a song, or a sudden absence. And then you realise the healing never happened. You simply stopped acknowledging and talking about it.

I chose a different route. I chose to face what happened—to sit with it, to understand it, and to work toward letting it go. To turn the pain of separation into something that might one day resemble peace, shaped not by denial, but by acceptance.

This wasn't the easier path. It was the hardest. So, to anyone who says, "just get on with it," I offer this truth: burying pain isn't resilience—it's postponement. Real strength is found in the slow, vulnerable work of healing. In doing the uncomfortable inner work so the damage doesn't pass on. In reclaiming your own story, not letting someone else's choices write the ending.

I won't live bitter. I won't define my life by what I've lost. And I will never surrender my role as a father—and will choose presence over silence, courage over avoidance, and peace over pretense.

I awoke the next morning in my Perth townhouse—my old world. The familiar walls felt distant now, the space too large, too quiet. It was no longer home in the way it once was. I had changed in New Zealand. Something inside me had shifted—freed, softened, expanded. I had found a deeper truth in simplicity, solitude, and nature.

I was now a man at peace. A man who wanted less but felt more. Extravagance no longer appealed to me—it had been a marker of a former life, a former self. I thought of Michaela that morning. Of what might have been had we stayed on the old path. I still miss her some days—how could I not? But now, there's a quiet relief in knowing things unfolded as they did.

I have space now. Space for reconnection. Space for closeness with my kids, unburdened by compromise or distraction. Space for heart—mine, and Jonas's too. Because now, I know they are one and the same.

I'm friendly with Michaela. At the time of writing, we spoke. She's moved on into a new relationship, and I'm genuinely happy for her. I get the sense she feels the same for me—that there's mutual goodwill as we each continue along our separate paths.

There's a quiet recognition, I think, on both sides. A shared understanding that what we had was meaningful, even if it couldn't last forever in the form we once knew. The love was real, but the circumstances were too complex, too burdened. Still, I hope a friendship between us endures. One built on respect, shared history, and a tenderness that remains even when the romantic chapter has closed. Michaela was, and will always be, one of my most cherished angels. She entered my life at a time I was drowning and gave me reason to breathe again. For that—and so much more—I'll never forget her.

The following evening, I'd arranged to take Olivia out for dinner. Indian—her favourite. Plenty of papadums, mango lassi, butter chicken, and of course, garlic naan.

Sitting in my van parked outside the familiar driveway, I found myself remembering the years of monotonous agony—those countless drop-offs, the lump in my throat each time I saw Wayne's car parked there, his presence always just out of view, safely hidden behind the brick walls. But this time, something had shifted. I smiled, not with bitterness, but with calm. My heart was focused now on rebuilding the beautiful relationship I still had with my daughter. Peace had taken the place of resentment.

I even felt a degree of pity for Wayne. A man caught in a dynamic he probably never fully understood. A man who had never grasped the depth of a biological father's unwavering love. I didn't envy him. I no longer needed to.

Then I saw her—my beautiful Olivia, walking toward me. Her head tilted down before she glanced up to meet my gaze. That single glance lit something warm inside me. The feeling I used to have every time she came to my door, Arnie the dog tucked under one arm, schoolbag hanging from the other. She opened the van door, climbed in, and I leaned over to wrap her in a long, firm hug.

"Hey, Pos. Love you," I said. "You too, Dad," she whispered back, her voice soft and true. Just then, a black SUV pulled into the driveway. It was Dianne. I hadn't seen her in years—not since the failed counselling meeting. I looked over at Olivia. "Watch this," I said gently. "I'm going to go and hug your mum."

"No," she said quickly, her eyes wide with concern. Her fear was palpable—a fear that it might go wrong, erupt, or reopen old wounds. But I'd made a promise to Jonas. To myself. I would follow through on the message I received in the hotel room late one night—to listen to my heart no matter the risk.

I unbuckled my seatbelt, stepped out, and walked slowly up the driveway. Dianne was just getting out of the car, her back to me. "Hey Dianne," I said evenly, no edge in my voice. As she turned, I walked forward, arms open, smiling gently.

To my surprise, she smiled too—caught off guard—and met me halfway. We hugged. Briefly. Lightly. But it happened. After all those years. By then, Olivia had come closer, likely bracing for something else entirely. But there was nothing to fear. The past had softened from my stance. Our conversation lasted only a few minutes—light talk about life, work, and family—but it was real. It was enough. It was lovely.

When we got back into the car, both of us buckled in, I turned to Olivia and said quietly, "I'm sorry that took so many years, sweetheart." She looked at me, her eyes kind. "That's okay, Dad," she replied, smiling gently. And in that moment, everything felt lighter.

As I would soon discover, people move at their own pace when it comes to reconciliation—if they move at all. Jonas had warned me of a final test, and he was right.

It was a few weeks later, just before Olivia's eighteenth birthday, when she called me. We chatted about her party plans—she was going bowling with friends, and her voice brimmed with excitement. Hearing her so genuinely happy made my heart swell with pride. I thought of her journey—how much she'd overcome since birth, the hurdles she'd faced with quiet determination, and how she'd grown into this beautiful, emotionally intelligent, resilient young woman.

"Would you like me to come, sweetheart?" I asked, knowing there might be other considerations tugging at her—namely, her mother's feelings about my presence.

"Sure. It would be great, Dad. You can meet my friends and even my boyfriend," she replied without hesitation.

Her response lifted me. She was choosing joy, choosing her own moment. And why wouldn't she want her dad at her eighteenth? I was stoked—grateful to be included in a milestone I'd feared I might miss.

But a few days later, the tone shifted. Olivia called again, and this time, there was a long pause on the line. Silence. A weight in her voice I hadn't heard in our previous call. I could sense what she was struggling to say, so I helped her.

"Do you still want me at your birthday, sweetheart?" I asked gently, knowing the answer, but also knowing the pressure she was under.

"Well yes… but Mum's not really keen on the idea," she said softly.

Empathy struck me instantly—not just for myself, but for her. She was caught in the middle, trying to honour her own wishes while balancing the emotions of others still, ten years after her traditional family was torn apart. Her feelings deserved to be central on her birthday, but it was clear that wasn't how things were unfolding.

I replied calmly, "It's your birthday, Pos, and your feelings matter the most. If you want me there, I'll be there. Your mum may have her own views, and that's okay, but I'll text and email to let her know. I'll send you a message once I've done so, so you're not caught in between."

"Okay," she said quietly.

"I love you, Pos. Chat soon."

"Bye, Dad."

This is what follows…

"Hi Dianne,

I'll be seeing Olivia on her 18th Birthday. She'd like me as her father to share her celebratory experience. She's phoned me a few times wanting me to be there to meet her friends and be there as her dad. Olivia has informed me today of your lack of support on this. It's time to move past the control and support Olivia on her special day in this regard. It would also be prudent for Wayne to contact me prior to Monday evening so that he's not uncomfortable seeing me for the first time after my offer of goodwill has been rejected in the past. Give me a call if you like.

Kind regards, Mark Woodley"

I waited anxiously the next day, hopeful but realistic, knowing the most likely outcome. Still, I had given Olivia the chance—however slim—to include her dad at her eighteenth birthday celebration. I checked my phone repeatedly for a text, unsure whether my ex-wife had even received my message. Our last communication—months earlier—had ended with her saying she would block my number, so I turned instead to my email.

There it was.

The subject line was neutral, but the contents weren't. I opened, knowing from experience to read between the lines. The message carried a list of grievances—personal and historical—toward me, including a statement that staggered me: "Olivia has assured me she doesn't want you at her birthday party." The email went on to say that I was causing our daughter "unwanted stress", around her birthday.

I stared at the screen, stunned. Just days earlier, Olivia had been excited to introduce me to her friends—even her boyfriend. Now, I was being told she didn't want me there at all. The shift felt jarring, and I couldn't ignore the sense that she had been caught between her own feelings and the emotions of others close to her. I knew Olivia. Her heart was kind, loyal. If she was now saying the opposite of what she'd told me, I had to consider that she might be trying to manage someone else's distress, not her own.

A line from the message stood out with weight: "I will be monitoring Olivia's phone." The words hit me harder than I expected. They implied my ability to respond to Olivia or reassure her that I'd respect her wishes and celebrate with her another time—on her terms—might now be limited or even prevented. I leaned back, the laptop screen still open, a heavy silence pressing against the room.

Just days earlier, I had stood in her driveway, offering a hug to my ex-wife after years of conflict. It had been brief, spontaneous, even hopeful. We'd exchanged smiles and a few words like two people who had once shared a life and even kids. Now, this message felt like a harsh return to old patterns.

But something stopped me from falling back into bitterness.

Jonas's voice echoed in my thoughts, reminding me of the final test—the one I had been preparing for since the mountain. "Empathy," I whispered aloud, almost as a prayer. My breath slowed. My shoulders softened. I realised that this was the moment. The chance to choose something different. Not reaction. Not resentment. But empathy—for Olivia, caught in the middle and empathy for my ex-wife, whose own unresolved pain seemed to still be shaping the present.

The frustration inside me faded. I could feel it—this time, I had passed the test. Just as Olivia would come into adulthood and gradually form her own truths, I had come to mine. I would honour her journey by stepping aside with grace and waiting patiently for the right moments of connection, without blame or demand.

Like the clouds parting to reveal the mountain peak, time too would uncover what needed to be seen. Not by force, not with fury—but with quiet certainty.

I took another breath, thinking of my dear daughter caught between loyalties. Olivia, like Luke, would one day form her own truth. I could already see signs of that strength emerging in Luke, now excelling in his apprenticeship and full of purpose. I was proud of him—deeply proud.

The morning of Olivia's eighteenth birthday arrived. I called, hoping to hear her voice, to wish her a happy birthday in the simplest, most human way. But all I got was voicemail: *"Sorry, the person you have called is not available. Please leave a short 10-second message after the tone and we'll send the message as a text."* And that was it. That was the extent of our communication that day.

It was a hard reminder of the struggle to remain relevant in my daughter's life—something I had experienced in waves over the past ten years. I imagined what nature might do to someone who stood between a father and his child. But then I heard it again: Jonas's voice—my heart's voice—whispering: *"Empathy, Mark."* So, I breathed. Deep compassion would be the antidote. Without it, I risked becoming poisoned by the very pain I hoped to transform.

I thought back to the recent moment when I hugged my ex-wife. She seemed frustrated at times in conversation. I listened with surprise, recalling the life we once had. Private schools, five-star travel, comfort. A life I had worked hard to create. Yes, it came with stress, but it was fuelled by hope and ambition. I don't believe that life is all about constant happiness—it's not sustainable. But there is a deeper joy in navigating the highs and lows with acceptance. That was the lesson I had come to understand: happiness is fleeting. Peace is the true reward.

And still, I held love for her—as the mother of our children. Despite the years and recent event of difficulty, I wished her health and longevity. Our children need both of us.

A few months after Olivia's birthday, I wrote Luke a letter. An apology. A recognition of the times I couldn't be the father I wanted to be—not because of a lack of love, but because I was broken in those years. The damage I sustained had left me impaired, but that pain was never greater than what he may have felt himself. My apology wasn't a bid for redemption. It was a father trying to honour his son by telling the truth.

Thankfully, Luke and I had resumed a warm and loving relationship. I'd also seen Olivia again shortly after her birthday. I took her out for a celebratory dinner—Indian, of course, her favourite. She radiated a quiet new maturity, and I could feel her stepping into adulthood, full of light and grace.

I realized that my journey—painful as it had been—was not in vain. Though my hopes for a traditional family had dissolved, what remained was something perhaps even more valuable: a deep, unshakable love and survival. A peace forged through fire. If my story could offer any kind of blueprint for my kids— how to grow through hardship, how to find resilience and grace—it would have been worth it.

Not everything works out. Pain is inevitable. But how we carry it matters.

Some couples aren't meant to stay together forever, even when they share children. I understand that now. What I believe, however, is that both biological parents deserve the opportunity to meet any new adult entering their children's lives when requested. It's a basic principle of human respect—to provide understanding, to ease the primal tensions that naturally arise. Denying that process does a disservice not only to the parent but to the children caught in between.

The decade of loss and longing no longer consumes me. What's left is a space ready for love, understanding, and compassion. I've come to see forgiveness not as approval of all that happened and continues—but as a choice to live in peace. I don't know what the future holds for my relationship with my children, with their mother, or even with Wayne, if he remains part of their lives. But I remain hopeful—for change, for healing, for possibility.

I am searching the South Island of New Zealand for a property where I can build a life grounded in peace, nature, and love—a place to one day share with those closest to me. My son and daughter, now young adults, will be welcome to visit when they're ready, to experience the life I had once dreamed of showing them fifteen years ago. This place will also be where I might one day bring or meet a future partner. I'll continue moving between Perth and the beautiful Southern Alps, carrying with me both memory and hope.

I'm just one of millions of separated fathers around the world who love their children unconditionally. Though my relationships with my kids was altered by decisions I didn't make, I chose to keep showing up. To keep loving them. And I will do so for the rest of my life.

The experience changed me—not back to who I was before, that version is gone—but into someone more resilient, more empathetic, more awake to life's beauty and its fragility. My fatherhood today doesn't look like what I imagined. But it remains my truest identity and my highest calling.

I've found peace and acceptance. But that doesn't mean I like all the outcomes. That should be obvious. It simply means I've found calm in the storm. I've stopped fighting a past I can't change, and instead, I've opened a new chapter. The agony that once tore through me for ten relentless years has softened into a grounded, pragmatic, and optimistic mindset. One rooted in honesty and emotional clarity. A mindset ready to live with full integrity—to be the best father I can be and to live the best version of my life from here forward.

A week after Olivia's eighteenth birthday—when I was unable to contact her—I felt something shift. Not rage or despair this time, but resilience. A quiet strength. I felt the spark of peace. Not redemption. A stillness born not from winning but from letting go.

It reinforced the absolute necessity of empathy—towards my ex-wife, towards Wayne, towards my kids as they find their way through the aftermath of our broken family. And toward myself, for having endured what I once believed would break me.

That empathy reminded me of something I felt toward my mother in her final days. Despite the distance that had grown between us—and the letter she once wrote disowning me—I stayed by her side until the end. A year before she passed, she found the courage to apologise for her effect on me. Not in words, but in quiet gestures of affection that said everything we both needed to hear.

As she slipped away, I whispered her favourite song, *Time to Say Goodbye* by Andrea Bocelli, doing my best to stay in tune. Her breath was laboured, punctuated by the soft gurgling that often comes near the end. Yet from time to time, her lips moved faintly. Even then, I knew she could feel my presence. Her doctor had said hearing is the last sense to go, and I believed it. In those still hours, every past wound between us seemed to dissolve. Whatever pain had driven her to push me away—I let it go. She may have disowned me in a moment of despair, but I chose to leave her with love.

My last words to Mum were simple: "Thank you." She was a good mother. She was my soccer coach as a kid, drove me around to athletic carnivals and hugged me when she was healthy. Yes, she was flawed. Sometimes very hurtful. But she loved me—in the only way she knew how. Her rejection of me wasn't cruelty. It was out of absolute pain. The agony of someone who had felt abandoned all her life—by others, and yes, at times, by me.

When I walked down the steps of the palliative care hospital, I was drenched in tears. But somewhere underneath the grief, I felt something else: peace. I flew back to Perth that same afternoon, carrying with me something I hadn't felt in years—relief she was out of pain and a relief a mother and son's parting was in love. Empathy had always been the answer. It just took ten years—and a mountain—to bring it back to the surface again.

Ironically, my ex-wife was partly right in the message she sent a decade ago: '…you will be happier in time…' In some ways, she was correct. With time came a deeper internal peace—and perhaps, in hindsight, even a quiet 'thank you' feels appropriate. Her decision, though devastating, gave me the space I needed to confront and begin healing the unresolved traumas of my past, but still as a devoted father.

So, if you, too, find yourself looking out over the ruins of the life you once built, remember this: the path forward exists. It's steep. It's painful. But it's real. I made it to continued fatherhood. I'm rebuilding loving, healthy relationships with my children. This new version of fatherhood may look nothing like what you'd envisioned. It will take more from you than you ever thought you had to give. And there will be times when moving forward feels impossible.

Move anyway.

One step. Then another.

Keep calling out for your children, even when they disappear into silence. They hear you, even if they don't know how to respond. Your love teaches them it's safe to return.

And your younger self—that innocent, wide-eyed child you used to be—needs to know that healing is possible. That suffering doesn't have to define a life. Let him see your survival.

Lean into your power of youthful innocence and stand in repair with empathy.

The summit lies ahead, not as a triumph but as a vision, an invitation to a new journey—a vantage point of perspective from which to view both where you've been and where you may yet travel. I'll meet you there.

Keep climbing.

Visit www.separatedfathersrecovery.com for more information

Young Mark